NONE DARE CALL IT
CONSPIRACY

BY GARY ALLEN

CONCORD

PRESS

Rossmoor, California

You may have received this book through the mail. It is a gift from a concerned American who has read the book. The donor believes that the survival of our country hinges on the public becoming aware of the material contained herein. All he asks is that you read the book. Thank you.

Gary Allen is a California based free-lance journalist. After majoring in history at Stanford University and doing graduate work at California State College at Long Beach, he became aware through independent research that his college courses had been highly slanted. Many of the most important facts had been left out. This book is the result of his personal "post graduate studies" in finding out "who's whose" in American politics.

First printing, February, 1972—350,000
Second printing, March, 1972—1,250,000

Published by
CONCORD PRESS
P. O. BOX 2686
SEAL BEACH, CALIF. 90740

Manufactured in the United States of America

TABLE OF CONTENTS

Chapter

One   Don't Confuse Me with Facts 7

Two   Socialism—Royal Road to Power For The
Super-Rich 17

Three   The Money Manipulators 36

Four   Bankrolling The Bolshevik Revolution 58

Five   Establishing The Establishment 78

Six   The Rockefellers And The Reds 98

Seven   Pressure From Above and Pressure From
Below 113

Eight   You Are The Answer 128

INTRODUCTION

The story you are about to read is true. The names have not been changed to protect the guilty. This book may have the effect of changing your life. After reading this book, you will never look at national and world events in the same way again.

None Dare Call It Conspiracy will be a very controversial book. At first it will receive little publicity and those whose plans are exposed in it will try to kill it by the silent treatment. For reasons that become obvious as you read this book, it will not be reviewed in all the "proper" places or be available on your local bookstand. However, there is nothing these people can do to stop a grass roots book distributing system. Eventually it will be necessary for the people and organizations named in this book to try to blunt its effect by attacking it or the author. They have a tremendous vested interest in keeping you from discovering what they are doing. And they have the big guns of the mass media at their disposal to fire the barrages at *None Dare Call It Conspiracy*.

By sheer volume, the "experts" will try to ridicule you out of investigating for yourself as to whether or not the information in this book is true. They will ignore the fact that the author admits that some of his ideas are conjecture because the people who know the truth are not about to confess. They will find a typographical error or argue some point that is open to debate. If necessary they will lie in order to protect themselves by smearing this book. Psychologically many people would prefer to believe those who pooh-pooh the information herein because we all like to ignore bad news. We do so at our own peril!

Having been a college instructor, a State Senator and now a Congressman, I have had experience with real professionals at putting up smokescreens to cover up their own actions by trying to destroy the accuser. I hope that you will read this book carefully and draw your own conclusions and not accept the opinions of those who of necessity must attempt to discredit the book. Your future may depend upon it.

October 25, 1971

JOHN G. SCHMITZ
UNITED STATES CONGRESSMAN

CHAPTER ONE

DON'T CONFUSE ME WITH FACTS

Most of us have had the experience, either as parents or youngsters, of trying to discover the "hidden picture" within another picture in a children's magazine. Usually you are shown a landscape with trees, bushes, flowers and other bits of nature. The caption reads something like this: "Concealed somewhere in this picture is a donkey pulling a cart with a boy in it. Can you find them?" Try as you might, usually you could not find the hidden picture until you turned to a page farther back in the magazine which would reveal how cleverly the artist had hidden it from us. If we study the landscape we realize that the whole picture was painted in such a way as to conceal the real picture within, and once we see the "real picture," it stands out like the proverbial painful digit.

We believe the picture painters of the mass media are artfully creating landscapes for us which deliberately hide the real picture. In this book we will show you how to discover the "hidden picture" in the landscapes presented to us daily through newspapers, radio and television. Once you can see through the camouflage, you will see the donkey, the cart and the boy who have been there all along.

Millions of Americans are concerned and frustrated over mishappenings in our nation. They feel that something is wrong, drastically wrong, but because of the picture painters they can't quite put their fingers on it.

Maybe you are one of those persons. Something is bugging you, but you aren't sure what. We keep electing new Presidents who seemingly promise faithfully to halt the world-wide Communist advance, put the blocks to extravagant government spending, douse the fires of inflation, put the economy on an even keel, reverse the trend which is turning the country into a moral sewer, and toss the criminals into the hoosegow where they belong. Yet, despite high hopes and glittering campaign promises, these problems continue to worsen no matter who is in office. Each new administration, whether it be Republican or Democrat, continues the same basic policies of the previous administration which it had so thoroughly denounced during the election campaign. It is considered poor form to mention this, but it is true nonetheless. Is there a plausible reason to explain why this happens? We are not supposed to think so. We are supposed to think it is all accidental and coincidental and that therefore there is nothing we can do about it.

FDR once said: "In politics, nothing happens by accident. If it happens, you can bet it was planned that way." He was in a good position to know. We believe that many of the major world events that are shaping our destinies occur because somebody or somebodies have planned them that way. If we were merely dealing with the law of averages, half of the events affecting our nation's well-being should be good for America. If we were dealing with mere incompetence, our leaders should occasionally make a mistake in our favor. We shall attempt to prove that we are not really dealing with coincidence or stupidity, but with planning and brilliance. This small book deals with that planning and brilliance and how it has shaped the foreign and domestic policies of the last six administrations. We hope it will explain matters which have up to now seemed inexplicable; that it will bring into sharp focus images which have been obscured by the landscape painters of the mass media.

Those who believe that major world events result from planning are laughed at for believing in the "conspiracy theory of history." Of course, no one in this modern day and age really believes in the conspiracy theory of history —except those who have taken the time to study the subject. When you think about it, there are really only two theories of history. Either things happen by accident neither planned nor caused by anybody, or they happen because they *are* planned and somebody causes them to happen. In reality, it is the "accidental theory of history" preached in the unhallowed Halls of Ivy which should be ridiculed. Otherwise, why does every recent administration make the same mistakes as the previous ones? Why do they repeat the errors of the past which produce inflation, depressions and war? Why does our State Department "stumble" from one Communist-aiding "blunder" to another? If you believe it is all an accident or the result of mysterious and unexplainable tides of history, you will be regarded as an "intellectual" who understands that we live in a complex world. If you believe that something like 32,496 consecutive coincidences over the past forty years stretches the law of averages a bit, you are a kook!

Why is it that virtually all "reputable" scholars and mass media columnists and commentators reject the cause and effect or conspiratorial theory of history? Primarily, most scholars follow the crowd in the academic world just as most women follow fashions. To buck the tide means social and professional ostracism. The same is true of the mass media. While professors and pontificators profess to be tolerant and broadminded, in practice it's strictly a one way street—with all traffic flowing left. A Maoist can be tolerated by Liberals of Ivory Towerland or by the Establishment's media pundits, but to be a conservative, and a conservative who propounds a conspiratorial view, is absolutely *verboten*. Better you should be a drunk at a national WCTU convention!

Secondly, these people have over the years acquired a strong vested emotional interest in their own errors. Their intellects and egos are totally committed to the accidental theory. Most people are highly reluctant to admit that they have been conned or have shown poor judgment. To inspect the evidence of the existence of a conspiracy guiding our political destiny from behind the scenes would force many of these people to repudiate a lifetime of accumulated opinions. It takes a person with strong character indeed to face the facts and admit he has been wrong even if it was because he was uninformed.

Such was the case with the author of this book. It was

9

only because he set out to prove the conservative anti-Communists wrong that he happened to end up writing this book. His initial reaction to the conservative point of view was one of suspicion and hostility; and it was only after many months of intensive research that he had to admit that he had been "conned."

Politicians and "intellectuals" are attracted to the concept that events are propelled by some mysterious tide of history or happen by accident. By this reasoning they hope to escape the blame when things go wrong.

Most intellectuals, pseudo and otherwise, deal with the conspiratorial theory of history simply by ignoring it. They never attempt to refute the evidence. It can't be refuted. If and when the silent treatment doesn't work, these "objective" scholars and mass media opinion molders resort to personal attacks, ridicule and satire. The personal attacks tend to divert attention from the facts which an author or speaker is trying to expose. The idea is to force the person exposing the conspiracy to stop the exposure and spend his time and effort defending himself.

However, the most effective weapons used against the conspiratorial theory of history are ridicule and satire. These extremely potent weapons can be cleverly used to avoid any honest attempt at refuting the facts. After all, nobody likes to be made fun of. Rather than be ridiculed most people will keep quiet; and, this subject certainly does lend itself to ridicule and satire. One technique which can be used is to expand the conspiracy to the extent it becomes absurd. For instance, our man from the Halls of Poison Ivy might say in a scoffingly arrogant tone, "I suppose you believe every liberal professor gets a telegram each morning from conspiracy headquarters containing his orders for the day's brainwashing of his students?" Some conspiratorialists do indeed overdraw the picture by expanding the conspiracy (from the small clique which it is) to include every local knee-jerk liberal activist and government bureaucrat. Or, because of racial or religious bigotry, they will take small fragments of legitimate evidence and expand them into a conclusion that will support their par-

10

ticular prejudice, i.e., the conspiracy is totally "Jewish," "Catholic," or "Masonic." These people do not help to expose the conspiracy, but, sadly play into the hands of those who want the public to believe that all conspiratorialists are screwballs.

"Intellectuals" are fond of mouthing cliches like: "The conspiracy theory is often tempting. However, it is overly simplistic." To ascribe absolutely everything that happens to the machinations of a small group of power hungry conspirators *is* overly simplistic. But, in our opinion nothing is more simplistic than doggedly holding onto the accidental view of major world events.

In most cases Liberals simply accuse all those who discuss the conspiracy of being paranoid. "Ah, you right wingers," they say, "rustling every bush, kicking over every rock, looking for imaginary boogeymen." Then comes the *coup de grace*—labeling the conspiratorial theory as the "devil theory of history." The Liberals love that one. Even though it is an empty phrase, it sounds so sophisticated!

With the leaders of the academic and communications world assuming this sneering attitude towards the conspiratorial (or cause and effect) theory of history, it is not surprising that millions of innocent and well-meaning people, in a natural desire not to appear naive, assume the attitudes and repeat the cliches of the opinion makers. These persons, in their attempt to appear sophisticated, assume their mentors' air of smug superiority even though they themselves have not spent five minutes in study on the subject of international conspiracy.

The "accidentalists" would have us believe that ascribing any of our problems to planning is "simplistic" and all our problems are caused by Poverty, Ignorance and Disease—hereinafter abbreviated as PID. They ignore the fact that organized conspirators use PID, real and imagined, as an excuse to build a jail for us all. Most of the world has been in PID since time immemorial and it takes incredibly superficial thinking to ascribe the ricocheting of the United States government from one disaster

11

to another over the past thirty years to PID. "Accidental-ists" ignore the fact that some of the more advanced nations in the world have been captured by Communists. Czechoslovakia was one of the world's most modern industrial nations and Cuba had the second highest per capita income of any nation in Central and South America.

It is not true, however, to state that there are no members of the intellectual elite who subscribe to the conspiratorial theory of history. For example, there is Professor Carroll Quigley of the Foreign Service School at Georgetown University. Professor Quigley can hardly be accused of being a "right wing extremist." (Those three words have been made inseparable by the mass media.) Dr. Quigley has all the "liberal" credentials, having taught at the Liberal Establishment's academic Meccas of Princeton and Harvard. In his 1300-page, 8 pound tome *Tragedy and Hope,* Dr. Quigley reveals the existence of the conspiratorial network which will be discussed in this book. The Professor is not merely formulating a theory, but revealing this network's existence from firsthand experience. He also makes it clear that it is only the network's secrecy and not their goals to which he objects. Professor Quigley discloses:

> "I know of the operations of this network because I have studied it for twenty years and was permitted for two years, in the early 1960's, to examine its papers and secret records. I HAVE NO AVERSION TO IT OR TO MOST OF ITS AIMS AND HAVE, FOR MUCH OF MY LIFE, BEEN CLOSE TO IT AND TO MANY OF ITS INSTRUMENTS. I have objected, both in the past and recently, to a few of its policies . . . but in general my chief difference of opinion is that IT WISHES TO REMAIN UN-KNOWN, and I believe its role in history is significant enough to be known." (Emphasis added)

We agree, its role in history does deserve to be known. That is why we have written this book. However, we most

12

emphatically disagree with this network's aim which the Professor describes as "nothing less than to create a world system of financial control in private hands able to dominate the political system of each country and the economy of the world as a whole." In other words, this power mad clique wants to control and rule the world. Even more frightening, they want total control over all individual actions. As Professor Quigley observes: ". . . his [the individual's] freedom and choice will be controlled within very narrow alternatives by the fact that he will be numbered from birth and followed, as a number, through his educational training, his required military or other public service, his tax contributions, his health and medical requirements, and his final retirement and death benefits." It wants control over all natural resources, business, banking and transportation by controlling the governments of the world. In order to accomplish these aims the conspirators have had no qualms about fomenting wars, depressions and hatred. They want a monopoly which would eliminate all competitors and destroy the free enterprise system. And Professor Quigley, of Harvard, Princeton and Georgetown *approves!*

Professor Quigley is not the only academic who is aware of the existence of a clique of self-perpetuating conspirators whom we shall call *Insiders*. Other honest scholars finding the same individuals at the scenes of disastrous political fires over and over again have concluded that there is obviously an organization of pyromaniacs at work in the world. But these intellectually honest scholars realize that if they challenged the *Insiders* head-on, their careers would be destroyed. The author knows these men exist because he has been in contact with some of them.

There are also religious leaders who are aware of the existence of this conspiracy. In a UPI story dated December 27, 1965, Father Pedro Arrupe, head of the Jesuit Order of the Roman Catholic Church, made the following charges during his remarks to the Ecumenical Council:

"This . . . Godless society operates in an extremely

13

efficient manner at least in its higher levels of leadership. It makes use of every possible means at its disposal, be they scientific, technical, social or economic.

It follows a perfectly mapped-out strategy. It holds almost complete sway in international organizations, in financial circles, in the field of mass communications; press, cinema, radio and television."

There are a number of problems to be overcome in convincing a person of the possible existence of a conspiratorial clique of *Insiders* who from the very highest levels manipulate government policy. In this case truth is really stranger than fiction. We are dealing with history's greatest "whodunit," a mystery thriller which puts Erle Stanley Gardner to shame. If you love a mystery, you'll be fascinated with the study of the operations of the *Insiders*. If you do study this network of which Professor Quigley speaks, you will find that what had at first seemed incredible not only exists, but heavily influences our lives.

It must be remembered that the first job of any conspiracy, whether it be in politics, crime or within a business office, is to convince everyone else that no conspiracy exists. The conspirators success will be determined largely by their ability to do this. That the elite of the academic world and mass communications media always pooh-pooh the existence of the *Insiders* merely serves to camouflage their operations. These "artists" hide the boy, the cart and the donkey.

Probably at some time you have been involved with or had personal knowledge of some event which was reported in the news. Perhaps it concerned an athletic event, an election, a committee or your business. Did the report contain the "real" story, the story behind the story? Probably not. And for a variety of reasons. The reporter had time and space problems and there is a good chance the persons involved deliberately did not reveal all the facts. Possibly the reporter's own prejudices governed what facts went into the story and which were deleted. Our point is that most people know from personal experience that a news

14

story often is not the whole story. But many of us assume that our own case is unique when really it is typical. What is true about the reporting of local events is equally as true about the reporting of national and international events.

Psychological problems are also involved in inducing people to look at the evidence concerning the *Insiders*. People are usually comfortable with their old beliefs and conceptions. When Columbus told people the world was a ball and not a pancake, they were highly upset. They were being asked to reject their way of thinking of a lifetime and adopt a whole new outlook. The "intellectuals" of the day scoffed at Columbus and people were afraid they would lose social prestige if they listened to him. Many others just did not want to believe the world was round. It complicated too many things. And typical flat-earthers had such a vested interest involving their own egos, that they heaped abuse on Columbus for challenging their view of the universe. "Don't confuse us with facts; our minds are made up," they said.

These same factors apply today. Because the Establishment controls the media, anyone exposing the *Insiders* will be the recipient of a continuous fusillade of invective from newspapers, magazines, TV and radio. In this manner one is threatened with loss of "social respectability" if he dares broach the idea that there is organization behind any of the problems currently wracking America. Unfortunately, for many people social status comes before intellectual honesty. Although they would never admit it, social position is more important to many people than is the survival of freedom in America.

If you ask these people which is more important— social respectability or saving their children from slavery —they will tell you the latter, of course. But their actions (or lack of same) speak so much louder than their words. People have an infinite capacity for rationalization when it comes to refusing to face the threat to America's survival. Deep down these people are afraid they may be laughed at if they take a stand, or may be denied an invitation to some social climber's cocktail party. Instead of getting mad at the *Insiders,* these people actually get angry at those who are trying to save the country by exposing the conspirators.

One thing which makes it so hard for some socially minded people to assess the conspiratorial evidence objectively is that the conspirators come from the very highest social strata. They are immensely wealthy, highly educated and extremely cultured. Many of them have lifelong reputations for philanthropy. Nobody enjoys being put in the position of accusing prominent people of conspiring to enslave their fellow Americans, but the facts are inescapable. Many business and professional people are particularly vulnerable to the "don't jeopardize your social respectability" pitch given by those who don't want the conspiracy exposed. The *Insiders* know that if the business and professional community will not take a stand to save the private enterprise system, the socialism through which they intend to control the world will be inevitable. They believe that most business and professional men are too shallow and decadent, too status conscious, too tied up in the problems of their jobs and businesses to worry about what is going on in politics. These men are told that it might be bad for business or jeopardize their government contracts if they take a stand. They have been bribed into silence with their own tax monies!

We are hoping that the conspirators have underestimated the courage and patriotism remaining in the American people. We feel there are a sufficient number of you who are not mesmerized by the television set, who put God, family and country above social status, who will band together to expose and destroy the conspiracy of the *Insiders*. The philosopher Diogenes scoured the length and breadth of ancient Greece searching for an honest man. We are scouring the length and breadth of America in search of hundreds of thousands of intellecutally honest men and women who are willing to investigate facts and come to logical conclusions—no matter how unpleasant those conclusions may be.

16

CHAPTER TWO

SOCIALISM—ROYAL ROAD TO POWER FOR THE SUPER-RICH

Everyone knows that Adolph Hitler existed. No one disputes that. The terror and destruction that this madman inflicted upon the world are universally recognized. Hitler came from a poor family which had absolutely no social position. He was a high school drop-out and nobody ever accused him of being cultured. Yet this man tried to conquer the world. During his early career he sat in a cold garret and poured onto paper his ambitions to rule the world. We know that.

Similarly, we know that a man named Vladimir Ilich Lenin also existed. Like Hitler, Lenin did not spring from a family of social lions. The son of a petty bureaucrat, Lenin, who spent most of his adult life in poverty, has been responsible for the deaths of tens of millions of your fellow human beings and the enslavement of nearly a billion more. Like Hitler, Lenin sat up nights in a dank garret scheming how he could conquer the world. We know that too.

Is it not theoretically possible that a billionaire could be sitting, not in a garret, but in a penthouse, in Manhattan, London or Paris and dream the same dream as Lenin and Hitler? You will have to admit it is theoretically possible. Julius Caesar, a wealthy aristocrat, did. And such a man might form an alliance or association with other like-minded men, might he not? Caesar did. These men would be superbly educated, command immense social prestige and be able to pool astonishing amounts of money to carry out their purposes. These are advantages that Hitler and Lenin did not have.

It is difficult for the average individual to fathom such perverted lust for power. The typical person, of whatever nationality, wants only to enjoy success in his job, to be

17

able to afford a reasonably high standard of living complete with leisure and travel. He wants to provide for his family in sickness and in health and to give his children a sound education. His ambition stops there. He has no desire to exercise power over others, to conquer other lands or peoples, to be a king. He wants to mind his own business and enjoy life. Since he has no lust for power, it is difficult for him to imagine that there are others who have . . . others who march to a far different drum. But we must realize that there *have* been Hitlers and Lenins and Stalins and Caesars and Alexander the Greats throughout history. Why should we assume there are no such men today with perverted lusts for power? And if these men happen to be billionaires is it not possible that they would use men like Hitler and Lenin as pawns to seize power for themselves?

Indeed, difficult as this is to believe, such is the case. Like Columbus, we are faced with the task of convincing you that the world is not flat, as you had been led to believe all your life, but, instead, is round. We are going to present evidence that what you call "Communism" is not run from Moscow or Peking, but is an arm of a bigger conspiracy run from New York, London and Paris. The men at the apex of this movement are not Communists in the traditional sense of that term. They feel no loyalty to Moscow or Peking. They are loyal only to themselves and their undertaking. And these men certainly do not believe in the clap-trap pseudo-philosophy of Communism. They have no intention of dividing their wealth. Socialism is a philosophy which conspirators exploit, but in which only the naive believe. Just how finance capitalism is used as the anvil and Communism as the hammer to conquer the world will be explained in this book.

The concept that Communism is but an arm of a larger conspiracy has become increasingly apparent throughout the author's journalistic investigations. He has had the opportunity to interview privately four retired officers who spent their careers high in military intelligence. Much of what the author knows he learned from them. And the story is known to several thousand others. High military intelligence circles are well aware of this network. In addition, the author has interviewed six men who have spent considerable time as investigators for Congressional committees. In 1953, one of these men, Norman Dodd, headed the Reece Committee's investigation of tax-free foundations. When Mr. Dodd began delving into the role of international high finance in the world revolutionary movement, the investigation was killed on orders from the Eisenhower-occupied White House. According to Mr. Dodd, it is permissable to investigate the radical bomb throwers in the streets, but when you begin to trace their activities back to their origins in the "legitimate world," the political iron curtain slams down.

You can believe anything you want about Communism except that it is a conspiracy run by men from the respectable world. People will often say to an active anti-Communist: "I can understand your concern with Communism, but the idea that a Communist conspiracy is making great inroads in the United States is absurd. The American people are anti-Communist. They're not about to buy Communism. It's understandable to be concerned about Communism in Africa or Asia or South America with their tremendous poverty, ignorance and disease. But to be concerned about Communism in the United States where the vast majority of people have no sympathy with it whatsoever is a misspent concern."

On the face of it, that is a very logical and plausible argument. The American people are indeed anti-Communist. Suppose you were to lay this book down right now, pick up a clip board and head for the nearest shopping center to conduct a survey on Americans' attitudes about Communism. "Sir," you say to the first prospect you encounter, "we would like to know if you are for or against Communism?"

Most people would probably think you were putting them on. If we stick to our survey we would find that ninety-nine percent of the people are anti-Communist. We probably would be hard put to find anybody who would take an affirmative stand for Communism.

So, on the surface it appears that the charges made against anti-Communists concerned with the internal threat of Communism are valid. The American people are not pro-Communist. But before our imaginary interviewee walks away in disgust with what he believes is a hokey survey, you add: "Sir, before you leave there are a couple of other questions I would like to ask. You won't find these quite so insulting or ludicrous." Your next question is: "What is Communism? Will you define it, please?"

Immediately a whole new situation has developed. Rather than the near unanimity previously found, we now have an incredible diversity of ideas. There are a multitude of opinions on what Communism is. Some will say: "Oh, yes, Communism. Well, that's a tryannical brand of socialism." Others will maintain: "Communism as it was originally intended by Karl Marx was a good idea. But it has never been practiced and the Russians have loused it up." A more erudite type might proclaim: "Communism is simply a rebirth of Russian imperialism."

If perchance one of the men you asked to define Communism happened to be a political science professor from the local college, he might well reply: "You can't ask 'what is Communism?' That is a totally simplistic question about an extremely complex situation. Communism today, quite unlike the view held by the right wing extremists in America, is not an international monolithic movement. Rather, it is a polycentric, fragmented, nationalistic movement deriving its character through the charismas of its various national leaders. While, of course, there is the welding of Hegelian dialectics with Feuerbachian materialism held in common by the Communist parties generally, it is a monumental oversimplification to ask 'what is Communism.' Instead you should ask: What is the Communism of Mao Tse-tung? What is the Communism of the late Ho Chi Minh, or Fidel Castro or Marshal Tito?"

If you think we are being facetious here, you haven't

talked to a political science professor lately. For the above is the prevailing view on our campuses, not to mention in our State Department.

Whether you agree or disagree with any of these definitions, or, as may well be the case, you have one of your own, one thing is undeniable. No appreciable segment of the anti-Communist American public can agree on just what it is that they are against. Isn't that frightening? Here we have something that almost everybody agrees is bad, but we cannot agree on just what it is we are against.

How would this work in a football game, for example? Can you imagine how effective the defense of a football team would be if the front four could not agree with the linebackers who could not agree with the corner backs who could not agree with the safety men who could not agree with the assistant coaches who could not agree with the head coach as to what kind of defense they should put up against the offense being presented? The obvious result would be chaos. You could take a sand lot team and successfully pit them against the Green Bay Packers if the Packers couldn't agree on what it is they are opposing. That is academic. The first principle in any encounter, whether it be football or war (hot or cold), is: Know your enemy. The American people do not know their enemy. Consequently, it is not strange at all that for three decades we have been watching one country of the world after another fall behind the Communist curtain.

In keeping with the fact that almost everybody seems to have his own definition of Communism, we are going to give you ours, and then we will attempt to prove to you that it is the only valid one. Communism: AN INTERNATIONAL, CONSPIRATORIAL DRIVE FOR POWER ON THE PART OF MEN IN HIGH PLACES WILLING TO USE ANY MEANS TO BRING ABOUT THEIR DESIRED AIM—GLOBAL CONQUEST.

You will notice that we did not mention Marx, Engels, Lenin, Trotsky, bourgeois, proletariat or dialectical materialism. We said nothing of the pseudo-economics or political philosophy of the Communists. These are the

21

TECHNIQUES of Communism and should not be confused with the Communist conspiracy itself. We did call it an international conspiratorial drive for power. Unless we understand the conspiratorial nature of Communism, we don't understand it at all. We will be eternally fixated at the Gus Hall level of Communism. And that's not where it's at, baby!

The way to bring down the wrath of the Liberal press Establishment or the professional Liberals is simply to use the word *conspiracy* in relation to Communism. We are not supposed to believe that Communism is a political conspiracy. We can believe anything else we wish to about it. We can believe that it is brutal, tyrannical, evil or even that it intends to bury us, and we will win the plaudits of the vast majority of American people. But don't ever, ever use the word *conspiracy* if you expect applause, for that is when the wrath of Liberaldom will be unleashed against you. We are not disallowed from believing in *all* types of conspiracy, just modern political conspiracy.

We know that down through the annals of history small groups of men have existed who have conspired to bring the reins of power into their hands. History books are full of their schemes. Even *Life* magazine believes in conspiracies like the Cosa Nostra where men conspire to make money through crime. You may recall that *Life* did a series of articles on the testimony of Joseph Valachi before the McClellan Committee several years ago. There are some aspects of those revelations which are worth noting.

Most of us did not know the organization was called Cosa Nostra. Until Valachi "sang" we all thought it was named the Mafia. That is how little we knew about this group, despite the fact that it was a century old and had been operating in many countries with a self-perpetuating clique of leaders. We didn't even know it by its proper name. Is it not possible a political conspiracy might exist, waiting for a Joseph Valachi to testify? Is Dr. Carroll Quigley the Joseph Valachi of political conspiracies?

We see that everybody, even *Life* magazine, believes

in some sort of conspiracy. The question is: Which is the more lethal form of conspiracy—criminal or political? And what is the difference between a member of the Cosa Nostra and a Communist, or more properly, an *Insider* conspirator? Men like Lucky Luciano who have scratched and clawed to the top of the heap in organized crime must, of necessity, be diabolically brilliant, cunning and absolutely ruthless. But, almost without exception, the men in the hierarchy of organized crime have had no formal education. They were born into poverty and learned their trade in the back alleys of Naples, New York or Chicago.

Now suppose someone with this same amoral grasping personality were born into a patrician family of great wealth and was educated at the best prep schools, then Harvard, Yale or Princeton, followed by graduate work possibly at Oxford. In these institutions he would become totally familiar with history, economics, psychology, sociology and political science. After having graduated from such illustrious establishments of higher learning, are we likely to find him out on the streets peddling fifty cent tickets to a numbers game? Would you find him pushing marijuana to high schoolers or running a string of houses of prostitution? Would he be getting involved in gangland killings? Not at all. For with that sort of education, this person would realize that if one wants power, real power, the lessons of history say, "Get into the government business." Become a politician and work for political power or, better yet, get some politicians to front for you. That is where the real power—and the real money—is.

Conspiracy to seize the power of government is as old as government itself. We can study the conspiracies surrounding Alcibiades in Greece or Julius Caesar in ancient Rome, but we are not supposed to think that men today scheme to achieve political power.

Every conspirator has two things in common with every other conspirator. He must be an accomplished liar and a far-seeing planner. Whether you are studying Hitler, Alcibiades, Julius Caesar or some of our contemporary

23

conspirators, you will find that their patient planning is almost overwhelming. We repeat FDR's statement: "In politics, nothing happens by accident. If it happens, you can bet it was planned that way."

In reality, Communism is a tyranny planned by power seekers whose most effective weapon is the big lie. And if one takes all the lies of Communism and boils them down, you will find they distill into two major lies out of which all others spring. They are: (1) Communism is inevitable, and (2) Communism is a movement of the downtrodden masses rising up against exploiting bosses.

Let us go back to our imaginary survey and analyze our first big lie of Communism—that it is inevitable. You will recall that we asked our interviewee if he was for or against Communism and then we asked him to define it. Now we are going to ask him: "Sir, do you think Communism is inevitable in America?" And in almost every case the response will be something like this: "Oh, well, no. I don't think so. You know how Americans are. We are a little slow sometimes in reacting to danger. You remember Pearl Harbor. But the American people would never sit still for Communism."

Next we ask: "Well then, do you think socialism is inevitable in America?" The answer, in almost every case will be similar to this: "I'm no socialist, you understand, but I see what is going on in this country. Yeah, I'd have to say that socialism is inevitable."

Then we ask our interviewee: "Since you say you are not a socialist but you feel the country is being socialized, why don't you do something about it?" His response will run: "I'm only one person. Besides it's inevitable. You can't fight city hall, heh, heh, heh."

Don't you know that the boys down at city hall are doing everything they can to convince you of that? How effectively can you oppose anything if you feel your opposition is futile? Giving your opponent the idea that defending himself is futile is as old as warfare itself. In about 500 B. C. the Chinese war lord-philosopher Sun Tsu stated, "Supreme excellence in warfare lies in the destruction of your enemy's will to resist in advance of perceptible hostilities." We call it "psy war" or psychological warfare today. In poker, it is called "running a good bluff." The principle is the same.

Thus we have the American people: anti-Communist, but unable to define it and anti-socialist, but thinking it is inevitable. How did Marx view Communism? How important is "the inevitability of Communism" to the Communists? What do the Communists want you to believe is inevitable—Communism or socialism? If you study Marx' *Communist Manifesto* you will find that in essence Marx said the proletarian revolution would establish the SOCIALIST dictatorship of the proletariat. To achieve the SOCIALIST dictatorship of the proletariat, three things would have to be accomplished: (1) The elimination of all right to private property; (2) The dissolution of the family unit; and (3) Destruction of what Marx referred to as the "opiate of the people," religion.

Marx went on to state that when the dictatorship of the proletariat had accomplished these three things throughout the world, and after some undetermined length of time (as you can imagine, he was very vague on this point), the all powerful state would miraculously wither away and state socialism would give way to Communism. You wouldn't need any government at all. Everything would be peace, sweetness and light and everybody would live happily ever after. But first, all Communists must work to establish SOCIALISM.

Can't you just see Karl Marx really believing that an omnipotent state would wither away? Or can you imagine that a Joseph Stalin (or any other man with the cunning and ruthlessness necessary to rise to the top of the heap in an all-powerful dictatorship) would voluntarily dismantle the power he had built by fear and terror?*

(*Karl Marx was hired by a mysterious group who called themselves the League of Just Men to write the *Communist Manifesto* as demogogic boob-bait to appeal to the mob. In actual fact the *Communist Manifesto* was in circulation for many years before Marx' name was widely enough recognized to establish his authorship for this revolutionary handbook. All Karl Marx really did was to update and codify the very same revo-

25

Socialism would be the bait . . . the excuse to establish the dictatorship. Since dictatorship is hard to sell in idealistic terms, the idea had to be added that the dictatorship was just a temporary necessity and would soon dissolve of its own accord. You really have to be naive to swallow that, but millions do!

The drive to establish SOCIALISM, not Communism, is at the core of everything the Communists and the *Insiders* do. Marx and all of his successors in the Communist movement have ordered their followers to work on building SOCIALISM. If you go to hear an official Communist speaker, he never mentions Communism. He will speak only of the struggle to complete the socialization of America. If you go to a Communist bookstore you will find that all of their literature pushes this theme. It does *not* call for the establishment of Communism, but SOCIALISM.

And many members of the Establishment push this same theme. The September 1970 issue of *New York* magazine contains an article by Harvard Professor John Kenneth Galbraith, himself a professed socialist, entitled "Richard Nixon and the Great Socialist Revival." In describing what he calls the "Nixon Game Plan," Galbraith states:

"Mr. Nixon is probably not a great reader of Marx, but [his advisors] Drs. Burns, Shultz and McCracken are excellent scholars who know him well and could have brought the President abreast and it is beyond denying that the crisis that aided the rush into socialism was engineered by the Administration. . . ."

lutionary plans and principles set down seventy years earlier by Adam Weishaupt, the founder of the Order of Illuminati in Bavaria. And, it is widely acknowledged by serious scholars of this subject that the League of Just Men was simply an extension of the Illuminati which was forced to go deep underground after it was exposed by a raid in 1786 conducted by the Bavarian authorities.)

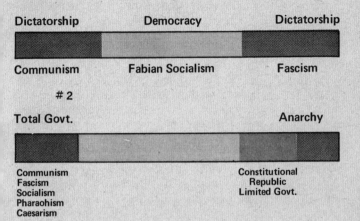

Chart 1 and 2

1

Dictatorship	Democracy	Dictatorship
Communism	Fabian Socialism	Fascism

2

Total Govt.   Anarchy

Communism   Constitutional
Fascism   Republic
Socialism   Limited Govt.
Pharaohism
Caesarism

Chart 1 depicts a false Left-Right political spectrum used by Liberals which has Communism (International Socialism) on the far Left and its twin, Fascism (National Socialism) on the far Right with the "middle of the road" being Fabian Socialism. The entire spectrum is Socialist!

Chart 2 is a more rational political spectrum with total government in any form on the far Left and no government or anarchy on the far right. The U. S. was a Republic with a limited government, but for the past 60 years we have been moving leftward across the spectrum towards total government with each new piece of socialist legislation.

There is an accurate political spectrum. (See Chart 2.) Communism is, by definition, total government. If you have total government it makes little difference whether you call it Communism, Fascism, Socialism, Caesarism or Pharaohism. It's all pretty much the same from the standpoint of the people who must live and suffer under it. If total government (by any of its pseudonyms) stands on the far Left, then by logic the far Right should represent anarchy, or no government.

Our Founding Fathers revolted against the near-total government of the English monarchy. But they knew that having no government at all would lead to chaos. So they set up a Constitutional Republic with a very limited government. They knew that men prospered in freedom. Although the free enterprise system is not mentioned specifically in the Constitution, it is the only one which can exist under a Constitutional Republic. All collectivist systems require power in government which the Constitution did not grant. Our Founding Fathers had no intention of allowing the government to become an instrument to steal the fruit of one man's labor and give it to another who had not earned it. Our government was to be one of severely limited powers. Thomas Jefferson said: "In questions of power then let no more be heard of confidence in man, but bind him down from mischief by the chains of the Constitution." Jefferson knew that if the government were not enslaved, people soon would be.

It was Jefferson's view that government governs best which governs least. Our forefathers established this country with the very least possible amount of government. Although they lived in an age before automobiles, electric lights and television, they understood human nature and its relation to political systems far better than do most Americans today. Times change, technology changes, but principles are eternal. Primarily, government was to provide for national defense and to establish a court system. But we have burst the chains that Jefferson spoke of and for many years now we have been moving leftward across the political spectrum toward collectivist total government. Every proposal by our political leaders (including some which are supposed to have the very opposite effect, such as Nixon's revenue sharing proposal) carries us further leftward to centralized government. This is not because socialism is inevitable. It is no more inevitable than Pharaohism. It is largely the result of clever planning and patient gradualism.

Since all Communists and their *Insider* bosses are waging

a constant struggle for SOCIALISM, let us define that term. Socialism is usually defined as government ownership and/or control over the basic means of production and distribution of goods and services. When analyzed this means government control over everything, including you. All controls are "people" controls. If the government controls these areas it can eventually do just exactly as Marx set out to do—destroy the right to private property, eliminate the family and wipe out religion.

We are being socialized in America and everybody knows it. If we had a chance to sit down and have a cup of coffee with the man in the street that we have been interviewing, he might say: "You know, the one thing I can never figure out is why all these very, very wealthy people like the Kennedys, the Fords, the Rockefellers and others are for socialism. Why are the super-rich for socialism? Don't they have the most to lose? I take a look at my bank account and compare it with Nelson Rockefeller's and it seems funny that I'm against socialism and he's out promoting it." Or is it funny? In reality, there is a vast difference between what the promoters define as socialism and what it is in actual practice. The idea that socialism is a share-the-wealth program is strictly a confidence game to get the people to surrender their freedom to an all-powerful collectivist government. While the *Insiders* tell us we are building a paradise on earth, we are actually constructing a jail for ourselves.

Doesn't it strike you as strange that some of the individuals pushing hardest for socialism have their own personal wealth protected in family trusts and tax-free foundations? Men like Rockefeller, Ford and Kennedy are for every socialist program known to man which will increase your taxes. Yet they pay little, if anything, in taxes themselves. An article published by the North American Newspaper Alliance in August of 1967 tells how the Rockefellers pay practically no income taxes despite their vast wealth. The article reveals that one of the Rockefellers paid the grand total of $685 personal income tax during a

31

recent year. The Kennedys have their Chicago Merchandise Mart, their mansions, yachts, planes etc., all owned by their myriads of family foundations and trusts. Taxes are for peons! Yet hypocrites like Rockefeller, Ford and Kennedy pose as great champions of the "downtrodden." If they were really concerned about the poor, rather than using socialism as a means of achieving personal political power, they would divest themselves of their own fortunes. There is no law which prevents them from giving away their own fortunes to the poverty stricken. Shouldn't these men set an example? And practice what they preach? If they advocate sharing the wealth, shouldn't they start with their own instead of that of the middle class which pays almost all the taxes? Why don't Nelson Rockefeller and Henry Ford II give away all their wealth, retaining only enough to place themselves at the national average? Can't you imagine Teddy Kennedy giving up his mansion, airplane and yacht and moving into a $25,000 home with a $20,000 mortgage like the rest of us?

We are usually told that this clique of super-rich are socialists because they have a guilt complex over wealth they inherited and did not earn. Again, they could relieve these supposed guilt complexes simply by divesting themselves of their unearned wealth. There are doubtless many wealthy do-gooders who have been given a guilt complex by their college professors, but that doesn't explain the actions of *Insiders* like the Rockefellers, Fords or Kennedys. All their actions betray them as power seekers.

But the Kennedys, Rockefellers and their super-rich confederates are not being hypocrites in advocating socialism. It appears to be a contradiction for the super-rich to work for socialism and the destruction of free enterprise. In reality it is not.

Our problem is that most of us believe socialism is what the socialists want us to believe it is—a share-the-wealth program. That is the theory. But is that how it works? Let us examine the only Socialist countries—according to the Socialist definition of the word—extant in

32

the world today. These are the Communist countries. The Communists themselves refer to these as Socialist countries, as in the Union of Soviet Socialist Republics. Here in the reality of socialism you have a tiny oligarchial clique at the top, usually numbering no more than three percent of the total population, controlling the total wealth, total production and the very lives of the other ninety-seven percent. Certainly even the most naive observe that Mr. Brezhnev doesn't live like one of the poor peasants out on the great Russian steppes. But, according to socialist theory, he is supposed to do just that!

If one understands that socialism is not a share-the-wealth program, but is in reality a method to *consolidate* and *control* the wealth, then the seeming paradox of super-rich men promoting socialism becomes no paradox at all. Instead it becomes the logical, even the perfect tool of power-seeking megalomaniacs. Communism, or more accurately, socialism, is not a movement of the downtrodden masses, but of the economic elite. The plan of the conspirator *Insiders* then is to socialize the United States, not to Communize it.

How is this to be accomplished? Chart 3 shows the structure of our government as established by our Founding Fathers. The Constitution fractionalized and subdivided governmental power in every way possible. The Founding Fathers believed that each branch of the government, whether at the federal, state or local level, would be jealous of its powers and would never surrender them to centralized control. Also, many phases of our lives (such as charity and education) were put totally, or almost totally, out of the grasp of politicians. *Under this system you could not have a dictatorship*. No segment of government could possibly amass enough power to form a dictatorship. In order to have a dictatorship one must have a single branch holding most of the reins of power. Once you have this, a dictatorship is inevitable.

Chart 3

CONSTITUTIONAL REPUBLIC

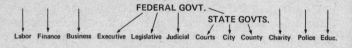

FEDERAL GOVT.

STATE GOVTS.

Labor   Finance   Business   Executive   Legislative   Judicial   Courts   City   County   Charity   Police   Educ.

DEMOCRATIC SOCIALISM

EXECUTIVE

Labor   Finance   Business   Legislative   Judicial   States   Counties   Cities   Charity   Police   Educ.

A dictatorship was impossible in our Republic because power was widely diffused. Today, as we approach Democratic Socialism, all power is being centralized at the apex of the executive branch of the federal government. This concentration of power makes a dictatorship inevitable. Those who control the President indirectly gain virtual control of the whole country.

The English philosopher Thomas Hobbes noted: "Freedom is government divided into small fragments." Woodrow Wilson, before he became the tool of the *Insiders,* observed: "This history of liberty is a history of the limitations of governmental power, not the increase of it." And the English historian Lord Acton commented: "Power tends to corrupt and absolute power corrupts absolutely." Even though these men lived after our Constitution was written, our forefathers understood these principles completely.

But what is happening today? As we move leftward along the political spectrum towards socialism, all the reins of power are being centralized in the executive branch of the federal government. Much of this is being done by buying with legislation or with "free" federal grants all the other entities. Money is used as bait and the hook is federal control. The Supreme Court has ruled, and in this case quite logically, that "it is hardly lack of due process for the government to regulate that which it subsidizes."

If you and your clique wanted control over the United States, it would be impossible to take over every city hall, county seat and state house. You would want all power vested at the apex of the executive branch of the federal government; then you would have only to control one man to control the whole shebang. If you wanted to control the nation's manufacturing, commerce, finance, transportation and natural resources, you would need only to control the apex, the power pinnacle, of an all-powerful SOCIALIST government. Then you would have a monopoly and could squeeze out all your competitors. If you want a national monopoly, you must control a national socialist government. If you want a worldwide monopoly, you must control a world socialist government. That is what the game is all about. "Communism" is not a movement of the downtrodden masses but is a movement created, manipulated and used by power-seeking billionaires in order to gain control over the world . . . first by establishing socialist governments in the various nations and then consolidating them all through a "Great Merger," into an all-powerful world socialist super-state probably under the auspices of the United Nations. The balance of this book will outline just how they have used Communism to approach that goal.

CHAPTER THREE

THE MONEY MANIPULATORS

Many college history professors tell their charges that the books they will be using in the class are "objective." But stop and ask yourself: Is it possible to write a history book without a particular point of view? There are billions of events which take place in the world each day. To think of writing a complete history of a nation covering even a year is absolutely incredible.

Not only is a historian's ability to write an "objective" history limited by the sheer volume of happenings but by the fact that many of the most important happenings never appear in the papers or even in somebody's memoirs. The decisions reached by the "Big Boys" in the smoked-filled rooms are not reported even in the *New York Times* which ostensibly reports all the news that is fit to print. ("All the news that fits" is a more accurate description.)

In order to build his case, a historian must select a miniscule number of facts from the limited number that are known. If he does not have a "theory," how does he separate important facts from unimportant ones? As Professor Stuart Crane has pointed out, this is why every book "proves" the author's thesis. But no book is objective. No book can be objective; and this book is not objective. (Liberal reviewers should have a ball quoting that out of context.) The information in it is true, but the book is not objective. We have carefully selected the facts to prove our case. We believe that most other historians have focused on the landscape, and ignored that which is most important: the cart, boy and donkey.

Most of the facts which we bring out are readily verifiable at any large library. But our contention is that we have arranged these facts in the order which most accurately reveals their true significance in history. These are the facts the Establishment does not want you to know.

Have you ever had the experience of walking into a mystery movie two-thirds of the way through? Confusing wasn't it? All the evidence made it look as if the butler were the murderer, but in the final scenes you find out, surprisingly, that it was the man's wife all along. You have to stay and see the beginning of the film. Then as all the pieces fall into place, the story makes sense.

This situation is very similar to the one in which millions of Americans find themselves today. They are confused by current happenings in the nation. They have come in as the movie, so to speak, is going into its conclusion. The earlier portion of the mystery is needed to make the whole thing understandable. (Actually, we are not really starting at the beginning, but we are going back far enough to give meaning to today's happenings.)

In order to understand the conspiracy it is necessary to have some rudimentary knowledge of banking and, particularly, of international bankers. While it would be an over-simplification to ascribe the entire conspiracy to international bankers, they nevertheless have played a key role. Think of the conspiracy as a hand with one finger labelled "international banking," others "foundations," "the anti-religion movement" "Fabian Socialism," and "Communism." But it was the international bankers of whom Professor Quigley was speaking when we quoted him earlier as stating that their aim was nothing less than control of the world through finance.

Where do governments get the enormous amounts of money they need? Most, of course, comes from taxation; but governments often spend more than they are willing to tax from their citizens and so are forced to borrow. Our national debt is now $455 billion—every cent of it borrowed at interest from somewhere.

The public is led to believe that our government borrows from "the people" through savings bonds. Actually, only the smallest percentage of the national debt is held by individuals in this form. Most government bonds, except those owned by the government itself through its trust funds, are held by vast banking firms known as international banks.

For centuries there has been big money to be made by international bankers in the financing of governments and kings. Such operators are faced, however, with certain thorny problems. We know that smaller banking operations protect themselves by taking collateral, but what kind of collateral can you get from a government or a king? What if the banker comes to collect and the king says, "Off with his head"? The process through which one collects a debt from a government or a monarch is not a subject taught in the business schools of our universities, and most of us—never having been in the business of financing kings—have not given the problem much thought. But there is a king-financing business and to those who can ensure collection it is lucrative indeed.

Economics Professor Stuart Crane notes that there are two means used to collateralize loans to governments and kings. Whenever a business firm borrows big money its creditor obtains a voice in management to protect his investment. Like a business, no government can borrow big money unless willing to surrender to the creditor some measure of sovereignty as collateral. Certainly international bankers who have loaned hundreds of billions of dollars to governments around the world command considerable influence in the policies of such governments.

But the ultimate advantage the creditor has over the king or president is that if the ruler gets out of line the banker can finance his enemy or rival. Therefore, if you want to stay in the lucrative king-financing business, it is wise to have an enemy or rival waiting in the wings to unseat every king or president to whom you lend. If the king doesn't have an enemy, you must create one.

Preeminent in playing this game was the famous House of Rothschild. Its founder, Meyer Amschel Rothschild (1743-1812) of Frankfurt, Germany, kept one of his five sons at home to run the Frankfurt bank and sent the others to London, Paris, Vienna and Naples. The Rothschilds became incredibly wealthy during the nineteenth century by financing governments to fight each other. According to Professor Stuart Crane:

> "If you will look back at every war in Europe during the Nineteenth Century, you will see that they always ended with the establishment of a 'balance of power.' With every re-shuffling there was a balance of power in a new grouping around the House of Rothschild in England, France, or Austria. They grouped nations so that if any king got out of line a war would break out and the war would be decided by which way the financing went. Researching the debt positions of the warring nations will usually indicate who was to be punished."

In describing the characteristics of the Rothschilds and other major international bankers, Dr. Quigley tells us that they remained different from ordinary bankers in several ways: they were cosmopolitan and international; they were close to governments and were particularly concerned with government debts, including foreign government debts; these bankers came to be called "international bankers." (Quigley, *Tragedy and Hope,* p. 52)

One major reason for the historical blackout on the role of the international bankers in political history is that the Rothschilds were Jewish. Anti-Semites have played into the hands of the conspiracy by trying to portray the entire conspiracy as Jewish. Nothing could be farther from the truth. The traditionally Anglo-Saxon J. P. Morgan and Rockefeller international banking institutions have played a key role in the conspiracy. But there is no denying the importance of the Rothschilds and their satellites. However, it is just as unreasonable and immoral to blame all Jews for the crimes of the Rothschilds as it is to hold all Baptists accountable for the crimes of the Rockefellers. The Jewish members of the conspiracy have used an organization called the Anti-Defamation League as an instrument to try to convince everyone that any mention of the Rothschilds or their allies is an attack on all Jews. In this way they have stifled almost all honest scholarship on international bankers and made the subject taboo within universities.

Any individual or book exploring this subject is immediately attacked by hundreds of A.D.L. committees all over the country. The A.D.L. has never let truth or logic interfere with its highly professional smear jobs. When no evidence is apparent, the A.D.L., which staunchly opposed so-called "McCarthyism," accuses people of being "latent anti-Semites." Can you imagine how they would yowl and scream if someone accused them of being "latent" Communists?

Actually, nobody has a right to be more angry at the Rothschild clique than their fellow Jews. The Warburgs, part of the Rothschild empire, helped finance Adolph Hitler. There were few if any Rothschilds or Warburgs in the Nazi prison camps! They sat out the war in luxurious hotels in Paris or emigrated to the United States or England. As a group, Jews have suffered most at the hands of these power seekers. A Rothschild has much more in common with a Rockefeller than he does with a tailor from Budapest or the Bronx.

Since the keystone of the international banking empires has been government bonds, it has been in the interest of these international bankers to encourage government debt. The higher the debt the more the interest. Nothing drives government deeply into debt like a war; and it has not been an uncommon practice among international bankers to finance both sides of the bloodiest military conflicts. For example, during our Civil War the North was financed by the Rothschilds through their American agent, August Belmont, and the American South through the Erlangers, Rothschild relatives.

But while wars and revolutions have been useful to international bankers in gaining or increasing control over

40

governments, the key to such control has always been control of money. You can control a government if you have it in your debt; a creditor is in a position to demand the privileges of monopoly from the sovereign. Money-seeking governments have granted monopolies in state banking, natural resources, oil concessions and transportation. However, the monopoly which the international financiers most covet is control over a nation's money.

Eventually these international bankers actually owned as private corporations the central banks of the various European nations. The Bank of England, Bank of France and Bank of Germany were not owned by their respective governments, as almost everyone imagines, but were privately owned monopolies granted by the heads of state, usually in return for loans. Under this system, observed Reginald McKenna, President of the Midlands Bank of England: "Those that create and issue the money and credit direct the policies of government and hold in their hands the destiny of the people." Once the government is in debt to the bankers it is at their mercy. A frightening example was cited by the *London Financial Times* of September 26, 1921, which revealed that even at that time: "Half a dozen men at the top of the Big Five Banks could upset the whole fabric of government finance by refraining from renewing Treasury Bills."

All those who have sought dictatorial control over modern nations have understood the necessity of a central bank. When the League of Just Men hired a hack revolutionary named Karl Marx to write a blueprint for conquest called *The Communist Manifesto,* the fifth plank read: "Centralization of credit in the hands of the state, by means of a national bank with state capital and an exclusive monopoly." Lenin later said that the establishment of a central bank was ninety percent of communizing a country. Such conspirators knew that you cannot take control of a nation without military force unless that nation has a central bank through which you can control its economy. The anarchist Bakunin sarcastically remarked about the followers of Karl Marx: "They have one foot in the bank and one foot in the socialist movement."

The international financiers set up their own front man in charge of each of Europe's central banks. Professor Quigley reports:

"It must not be felt that these heads of the world's chief central banks were themselves substantive powers in world finance. They were not. Rather, they were the technicians and agents of the dominant investment bankers of their own countries, who had raised them up and were perfectly capable of throwing them down. The substantive financial powers of the world were in the hands of these investment bankers (also called 'international' or 'merchants' bankers) who remained largely behind the scenes in their own unincorporated private banks. These formed a system of international cooperation and national dominance which was more private, more powerful, and more secret than that of their agents in the central banks. . . ." (Quigley, op. cit., pp. 326-7.)

Dr. Quigley also reveals that the international bankers who owned and controlled the Banks of England and France maintained their power even after those Banks were theoretically socialized.

Naturally those who controlled the central banks of Europe were eager from the start to fasten a similar establishment on the United States. From the earliest days, the Founding Fathers had been conscious of attempts to control America through money manipulation, and they carried on a running battle with the international bankers. Thomas Jefferson wrote to John Adams: ". . . I sincerely believe, with you, that banking establishments are more dangerous than standing armies. . . ."

But, even though America did not have a central bank after President Jackson abolished it in 1836, the European financiers and their American agents managed to obtain a great deal of control over our monetary system. Gustavus Myers, in his *History of The Great American Fortunes,* reveals:

> "Under the surface, the Rothschilds long had a powerful influence in dictating American financial laws. The law records show that they were powers in the old Bank of the United States [abolished by Andrew Jackson]."

During the nineteenth century the leading financiers of the metropolitan East often cut one another's financial throats, but as their Western and rural victims started to organize politically, the "robber barons" saw that they had a "community of interest" toward which they must work together to protect themselves from thousands of irate farmers and up and coming competitors. This diffusion of economic power was one of the main factors stimulating the demands for a central bank by would-be business and financial monopolists.

In *Years of Plunder* Proctor Hansl writes of this era:

> "Among the Morgans, Kuhn-Loebs and other similar pillars of the industrial order there was less disposition to become involved in disagreements that led to financial dislocation. A community of interest came into being, with results that were highly beneficial. . . ."

But aside from the major Eastern centers, most American bankers and their customers still distrusted the whole concept.

In order to show the hinterlands that they were going to need a central banking system, the international bankers created a series of panics as a demonstration of their power—a warning of what would happen unless the rest of the bankers got into line. The man in charge of conducting these lessons was J. Pierpont Morgan, American-born but educated in England and Germany. Morgan is referred to by many, including Congressman Louis Mc-Fadden, (a banker who for ten years headed the House Banking and Currency Committee), as the top American agent of the English Rothschilds.

By the turn of the century J. P. Morgan was already an old hand at creating artificial panics. Such affairs were well co-ordinated. Senator Robert Owen, a co-author of the Federal Reserve Act, (who later deeply regretted his role), testified before a Congressional Committee that the bank he owned received from the National Bankers' Association what came to be known as the "Panic Circular of 1893." It stated: "You will at once retire one-third of your circulation and call in one-half of your loans. . . ."

Historian Frederick Lewis Allen tells in *Life* magazine of April 25, 1949, of Morgan's role in spreading rumors about the insolvency of the Knickerbocker Bank and The Trust Company of America, which rumors triggered the 1907 panic. In answer to the question: "Did Morgan precipitate the panic?" Allen reports:

"Oakleigh Thorne, the president of that particular trust company, testified later before a congressional committee that his bank had been subjected to only moderate withdrawals . . . that he had not applied for help, and that it was the [Morgan's] 'sore point' statement alone that had caused the run on his bank. From this testimony, plus the disciplinary measures taken by the Clearing House against the Heinze, Morse and Thomas banks, plus other fragments of supposedly pertinent evidence, certain chroniclers have arrived at the ingenious conclusion that the Morgan interests took advantage of the unsettled conditions during the autumn of 1907 to precipitate the panic, guiding it shrewdly as it progressed so that it would kill off rival banks and consolidate the pre-eminence of the banks within the Morgan orbit."

The "panic" which Morgan had created, he proceeded

to end almost single-handedly. He had made his point. Frederick Allen explains:

"The lesson of the Panic of 1907 was clear, though not for some six years was it destined to be embodied in legislation: the United States gravely needed a central banking system. . . ."

The man who was to play the most significant part in providing America with that central bank was Paul Warburg, who along with his brother Felix had immigrated to the United States from Germany in 1902. (See Chart 4.) They left brother Max (later a major financier of the Russian Revolution) at home in Frankfurt to run the family bank (M. N. Warburg & Company).

Paul Warburg married Nina Loeb, daughter of Solomon Loeb of Kuhn, Loeb and Company, America's most powerful international banking firm. Brother Felix married Frieda Schiff, daughter of Jacob Schiff, the ruling power behind Kuhn, Loeb. Stephen Birmingham writes in his authoritative *Our Crowd*: "In the eighteenth century the Schiffs and Rothschilds shared a double house" in Frankfurt. Schiff reportedly bought his partnership in Kuhn, Loeb with Rothschild money.

Both Paul and Felix Warburg became partners in Kuhn, Loeb and Company.

In 1907, the year of the Morgan-precipitated panic, Paul Warburg began spending almost all of his time writing and lecturing on the need for "bank reform." Kuhn, Loeb and Company was sufficiently public spirited about the matter to keep him on salary at $500,000 per year while for the next six years he donated his time to "the public good."

Working with Warburg in promoting this "banking reform" was Nelson Aldrich, known as "Morgan's floor broker in the Senate." Aldrich's daughter Abby married John D. Rockefeller Jr. (the current Governor of New York is named for his maternal grandfather).

Chart 4
FEDERAL RESERVE

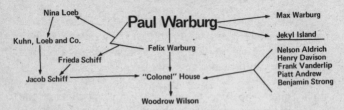

After the Panic of 1907, Aldrich was appointed by the Senate to head the National Monetary Commission. Although he had no technical knowledge of banking, Aldrich and his entourage spent nearly two years and $300,000 of the taxpayers' money being wined and dined by the owners of Europe's central banks as they toured the Continent "studying" central banking. When the Commission returned from its luxurious junket it held no meetings and made no report for nearly two years. But Senator Aldrich was busy "arranging" things. Together with Paul Warburg and other international bankers, he staged one of the most important secret meetings in the history of the United States. Rockefeller agent Frank Vanderlip admitted many years later in his memoirs:

"Despite my views about the value to society of greater publicity for the affairs of corporations, there was an occasion, near the close of 1910, when I was as secretive—indeed as furtive—as any conspirator . . . . I do not feel it is any exaggeration to speak of our secret expedition to Jekyl Island as the occasion of the actual conception of what eventaully became the Federal Reserve System."

The secrecy was well warranted. At stake was control over the entire economy. Senator Aldrich had issued confidential invitations to Henry P. Davison of J. P. Morgan & Company; Frank A. Vanderlip, President of the Rockefeller-owned National City Bank; A. Piatt Andrew, As-money were being made available, the mass media began to ballyhoo tales of the instant riches to be made in the stock market. According to Ferdinand Lundberg:

> "For profits to be made on these funds the public had to be induced to speculate, and it was so induced by misleading newspaper accounts, many of them bought and paid for by the brokers that operated the pools. . . ."

The House Hearings on Stabilization of the Purchasing Power of the Dollar disclosed evidence in 1928 that the Federal Reserve Board was working closely with the heads of European central banks. The Committee warned that a major crash had been planned in 1927. At a secret luncheon of the Federal Reserve Board and heads of the European central banks, the committee warned, the international bankers were tightening the noose.

Montagu Norman, Governor of the Bank of England, came to Washington on February 6, 1929, to confer with Andrew Mellon, Secretary of the Treasury. On November 11, 1927, the *Wall Street Journal* described Mr. Norman as "the currency dictator of Europe." Professor Carroll Quigley notes that Norman, a close confidant of J. P. Morgan, admitted: "I hold the hegemony of the world." Immediately after this mysterious visit, the Federal Reserve Board reversed its easy-money policy and began raising the discount rate. The balloon which had been inflated constantly for nearly seven years was about to be exploded.

On October 24, the feathers hit the fan. Writing in *The United States' Unresolved Monetary and Political Problems,* William Bryan describes what happened:

> "When everything was ready, the New York financiers started calling 24 hour broker call loans. This meant that the stock brokers and the customers had to dump their stock on the market in order to pay the loans. This naturally collapsed the stock market and brought a banking collapse all over the

And, curiously enough, the Federal Reserve System has never been audited and has firmly resisted all attempts by House Banking Committee Chairman Wright Patman to have it audited. *(N. Y. Times,* Sept. 14, 1967.)

How successful has the Federal Reserve System been? It depends on your point of view. Since Woodrow Wilson took his oath of office, the national debt has risen from $1 billion to $455 billion. The total amount of interest paid since then to the international bankers holding that debt, is staggering, with interest having become the third largest item in the federal budget. Interest on the national debt is now $22 billion every year, and climbing steeply as inflation pushes up the interest rate on government bonds. Meanwhile, our gold is mortgaged to European central banks, and our silver has all been sold. With economic catastrophe imminent, only a blind disciple of the "accidental theory of history" could believe that all of this has occurred by coincidence.

When the Federal Reserve System was foisted on an unsuspecting American public, there were absolute guarantees that there would be no more boom and bust economic cycles. The men who, behind the scenes, were pushing the central bank concept for the international bankers faithfully promised that from then on there would be only steady growth and perpetual prosperity. However, Congressman Charles A. Lindbergh Sr. accurately proclaimed: "From now on depressions will be scientifically created."

Using a central bank to create alternate periods of inflation and deflation, and thus whipsawing the public for vast profits, had been worked out by the international bankers to an exact science.

Having built the Federal Reserve as a tool to consolidate and control wealth, the international bankers were now ready to make a major killing. Between 1923 and 1929, the Federal Reserve expanded (inflated) the money supply by sixty-two percent. Much of this new money was used to bid the stock market up to dizzying heights.

At the same time that enormous amounts of credit

that the "money trust" had been defrocked should have been exploded when Paul Warburg was appointed to the first Federal Reserve Board—a board which was hand-picked by "Colonel" House. Paul Warburg relinquished his $500,000 a year job as a Kuhn, Loeb partner to take a $12,000 a year job with the Federal Reserve. The "accidentalists" who teach in our universities would have you believe that he did it because he was a "public spirited citizen." And the man who served as Chairman of the New York Federal Reserve Bank during its early critical years was the same Benjamin Strong of the Morgan interests, who accompanied Warburg, Davison, Vanderlip *et al.* to Jekyl Island, Georgia, to draft the Aldrich Bill.

How powerful is our "central bank?" The Federal Reserve controls our money supply and interest rates, and thereby manipulates the entire economy—creating inflation or deflation, recession or boom, and sending the market up or down at whim. The Federal Reserve powerful that Congressman Wright Patman, Chairman of the House Banking Committee, maintains:

> "In the United States today we have in effect two governments. . . . We have the duly constituted Government. . . . Then we have an independent, uncontrolled and uncoordinated government in the Federal Reserve System, operating the money powers which are reserved to Congress by the Constitution."

Neither Presidents, Congressmen nor Secretaries of the Treasury direct the Federal Reserve! In the matters of money, the Federal Reserve directs them! The uncontrolled power of the "Fed" was admitted by Secretary of the Treasury David M. Kennedy in an interview for the May 5, 1969, issue of *U. S. News & World Report*:

> "Q. Do you approve of the latest credit-tightening moves?
> A. It's not my job to approve or disapprove. It is the action of the Federal Reserve."

Prof. Carroll Quigley of Harvard, Princeton and Georgetown Universities wrote book disclosing international bankers' plan to control the world from behind the political and financial scenes. Quigley revealed plans of billionaires to establish dictatorship of the super-rich disguised as workers' democracies.

J. P. Morgan created artificial panic used as excuse to pass Federal Reserve Act. Morgan was instrumental in pushing U. S. into WWI to protect his loans to British government. He financed Socialist groups to create an all-powerful centralized government which international bankers would control at the apex from behind the scenes. After his death, his partners helped finance the Bolshevik Revolution in Russia.

country because the banks not owned by the oligarchy were heavily involved in broker call loans at this time, and bank runs soon exhausted their coin and currency and they had to close. The Federal Reserve System would not come to their aid, although they were instructed under the law to maintain an elastic currency."

The investing public, including most stock brokers and bankers, took a horrendous blow in the crash, but not the *Insiders*. They were either out of the market or had sold "short" so that they made enormous profits as the Dow Jones plummeted. For those who knew the score, a comment by Paul Warburg had provided the warning to sell. That signal came on March 9, 1929, when the *Financial Chronical* quoted Warburg as giving this sound advice:

"If orgies of unrestricted speculation are permitted to spread too far . . . the ultimate collapse is certain . . . to bring about a general depression involving the whole country."

Sharpies were later able to buy back these stocks at a ninety percent discount from their former highs.

To think that the scientifically engineered Crash of '29 was an accident or the result of stupidity defies all logic. The international bankers who promoted the inflationary policies and pushed the propaganda which pumped up the stock market represented too many generations of accumulated expertise to have blundered into "the great depression."

Congressman Louis McFadden, Chairman of the House Banking and Currency Committee, commented:

"It [the depression] was not accidental. It was a carefully contrived occurrence. . . . The international bankers sought to bring about a condition of despair here so that they might emerge as the rulers of us all."

Although we have not had another depression of the magnitude of that which followed 1929, we have since suffered regular recessions. Each of these has followed a period in which the Federal Reserve tromped down hard on the money accelerator and then slammed on the brakes. Since 1929 the following recessions have been created by such manipulation:

1936-1937—Stock prices fell fifty percent;

1948   —Stock prices dropped sixteen percent;

1953   —Stock declined thirteen percent;

1956-1957—The market dipped thirteen percent;

1957   —Late in the year the market plunged nine-teen percent;

1960   —The market was off seventeen percent;

1966   —Stock prices plummeted twenty-five percent;

1970   —The market plunged over twenty-five percent.

Chart 5, based on one appearing in the highly respected financial publication, *Indicator Digest* of June 24, 1969, shows the effects on the Dow-Jones Industrial Average of Federal Reserve policies of expanding or restricting the monetary supply. This is how the stock market is manipulated and how depressions or recessions are scientifically created. If you have inside knowledge as to which way the Federal Reserve policy is going to go, you can make a ton of money.

The members of the Federal Reserve Board are appointed by the President for fourteen year terms. Since these positions control the entire economy of the country they are far more important than cabinet positions, but who has ever heard of any of them except possibly Chairman Arthur Burns? These appointments which should be extensively debated by the Senate are routinely approved. But, here, as in Europe, these men are mere figureheads, put in their positions at the behest of the international

Chart 5

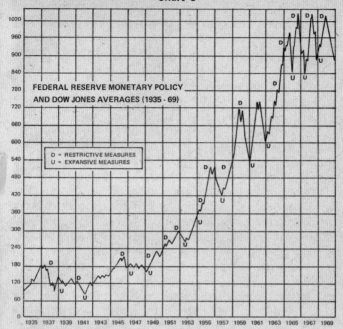

FEDERAL RESERVE MONETARY POLICY
AND DOW JONES AVERAGES (1935 - 69)

D = RESTRICTIVE MEASURES
U = EXPANSIVE MEASURES

bankers who finance the Presidential campaigns of both political parties.

And, Professor Quigley reveals that these international bankers who owned and controlled the Banks of England and France maintained their power even after those banks were theoretically socialized. The American system is slightly different, but the net effect is the same—ever-increasing debt requiring ever-increasing interest payments, inflation and periodic scientifically created depressions and recessions.

The end result, if the *Insiders* have their way, will be the dream of Montagu Norman of the Bank of England "that the Hegemony of World Finance should reign supreme over everyone, everywhere, as one whole supernational control mechanism." *(Montagu Norman* by John Hargrave, Greystone Press, N.Y., 1942.)

CHAPTER FOUR

BANKROLLING THE BOLSHEVIK REVOLUTION

The establishing of the Federal Reserve System provided the "conspiracy" with an instrument whereby the international bankers could run the national debt up to the sky, thereby collecting enormous amounts of interest and also gaining control over the borrower. During the Wilson Administration alone, the national debt expanded 800 percent.

Two months prior to the passage of the Federal Reserve Act, the conspirators had created the mechanism to collect the funds to pay the interest on the national debt. That mechanism was the progressive income tax, the second plank of Karl Marx' *Communist Manifesto* which contained ten planks for SOCIALIZING a country.

One quite naturally assumes that the graduated income tax would be opposed by the wealthy. The fact is that many of the wealthiest Americans supported it. Some, no doubt, out of altruism and because, at first, the taxes were very small. But others backed the scheme because they already had a plan for permanently avoiding both the income tax and the subsequent inheritance tax.

What happened was this: At the turn of the century the Populists, a group of rural socialists, were gaining strength and challenging the power of the New York bankers and monopolist industrialists. While the Populists had the wrong answers, they asked many of the right questions. Unfortunately, they were led to believe that the banker-monopolist control over government, which they opposed, was a product of free enterprise.

Since the Populist threat to the cartelists was from the Left (there being no organized political movement for *laissez-faire*), the *Insiders* moved to capture the Left. Professor Quigley discloses that over fifty years ago the Morgan firm decided to infiltrate the Leftwing political movement in the United States. This was not difficult to do since these Left groups needed funds and were eager for help to get their message to the public. Wall Street supplied both. There was nothing new about this decision, says Quigley, since other financiers had talked about it and even attempted it earlier. He continues:

> "What made it decisively important this time was the combination of its adoption by the dominant Wall Street financier, at a time when tax policy was driving all financiers to seek tax-exempt refuges for their fortunes. . . . " (Page 938)

Radical movements are never successful unless they attract big money and/or outside support. The great historian of the Twentieth Century, Oswald Spengler, was one of those who saw what American Liberals refuse to see—that the Left is controlled by its alleged enemy, the malefactors of great wealth. He wrote in his monumental *Decline of the West* (Modern Library, New York, 1945):

> "There is no proletarian, not even a Communist, movement, that has not operated in the interests of money, in the direction indicated by money, and for the time being permitted by money—and that without the idealists among its leaders having the slightest suspicion of the fact."

While the Populist movement was basically non-conspiratorial, its Leftist ideology and platform were made to order for the elitist *Insiders* because it aimed at concentrating power in government. The *Insiders* knew they could control that power and use it to their own purposes. They were not, of course, interested in promoting competition but in restricting it. Professor Gabriel Kolko has prepared a lengthy volume presenting the undeniable proof that the giant corporate manipulators *promoted* much of the so-called "progressive legislation" of the Roosevelt and Wilson eras—legislation which ostensibly was aimed at controlling their abuses, but which was so written as to suit their interests. In *The Triumph of Conservatism* (by which Kolko mistakenly means big business), he notes:

". . . the significant reason for many businessmen welcoming and working to increase federal intervention into their affairs has been virtually ignored by historians and economists. The oversight was due to the illusion that American industry was centralized and monopolized to such an extent that it could rationalize the activity [regulate production and prices] in its various branches voluntarily. Quite the opposite was true. Despite the large numbers of mergers, and the growth in the absolute size of many corporations, the dominant tendency in the American economy at the beginning of this century was toward growing competition. Competition was unacceptable to many key business and financial interests. . . ."

The best way for the *Insiders* to eliminate this growing competition was to impose a progressive income tax on their competitors while writing the laws so as to include built-in escape hatches for themselves. Actually, very few of the proponents of the graduated income tax realized they were playing into the hands of those they were seeking to control. As Ferdinand Lundberg notes in *The Rich And The Super-Rich:*

"What it [the income tax] became, finally, was a siphon gradually inserted into the pocketbooks of the general public. Imposed to popular huzzas as a class tax, the income tax was gradually turned into a mass tax in a jiujitsu turnaround. . . ."

The *Insiders'* principal mouthpiece in the Senate during this period was Nelson Aldrich, one of the conspirators involved in engineering the creation of the Federal Reserve and the maternal grandfather of Nelson Aldrich

Rockefeller. Lundberg says that "When Aldrich spoke, newsmen understood that although the words were his, the dramatic line was surely approved by 'Big John [D. Rockefeller]. . . .' " In earlier years Aldrich had denounced the income tax as "communistic and socialistic," but in 1909 he pulled a dramatic and stunning reversal. The *American Biographical Dictionary* comments:

> "Just when the opposition had become formidable he [Aldrich] took the wind out of its sails by bringing forward, with the support of the President [Taft], a proposed amendment to the Constitution empowering Congress to lay income taxes."

Howard Hinton records in his biography of Cordell Hull that Congressman Hull, who had been pushing in the House for the income tax, wrote this stunned observation:

> "During the past few weeks the unexpected spectacle of certain so-called 'old-line conservative' [sic] Republican leaders in Congress suddenly reversing their attitude of a lifetime and seemingly espousing, through ill-concealed reluctance, the proposed income-tax amendment to the Constitution has been the occasion of universal surprise and wonder."

The escape hatch for the *Insiders* to avoid paying taxes was ready. By the time the Amendment had been approved by the states (even before the income-tax was passed), the Rockefellers and Carnegie foundations were in full operation.

One must remember that it was to break up the Standard Oil (Rockefeller) and U. S. Steel (Carnegie) monopolies that the various anti-trust acts were ostensibly passed. These monopolists could now compound their wealth tax-free while competitors had to face a graduated income tax which made it difficult to amass capital. As we have said, socialism is not a share-the-wealth pro-

61

gram, as the socialists would like you to believe, but a consolidate-and-control-the-wealth program for the *Insiders.* The Reece Committee which investigated foundations for Congress in 1953 proved with an overwhelming amount of evidence that the various Rockefeller and Carnegie foundations have been promoting socialism since their inception. (See Rene Wormser's *Foundations: Their Power and Influence,* Devin Adair, New York, 1958.)

The conspirators now had created the mechanisms to run up the debt, to collect the debt, and (for themselves) to avoid the taxes required to pay the yearly interest on the debt. Then all that was needed was a reason to escalate the debt. Nothing runs up a national debt like a war. And World War I was being brewed in Europe.

In 1916, Woodrow Wilson was re-elected by a hair. He had based his campaign on the slogan: "He Kept Us Out of War!" The American public was extremely opposed to America's getting involved in a European war. Staying out of the perennial foreign quarrels had been an American tradition since George Washington. But as Wilson was stumping the country giving his solemn word that American soldiers would not be sent into a foreign war, he was perparing to do just the opposite. His "alter ego," as he called "Colonel" House, was making behind-the-scenes agreements with England which committed America to entering the war. Just five months later we were in it. The same crowd which manipulated the passage of the income tax and the Federal Reserve System wanted America in the war. J. P. Morgan, John D. Rockefeller, "Colonel" House, Jacob Schiff, Paul Warburg and the rest of the Jekyl Island conspirators were all deeply involved in getting us involved. Many of these financiers had loaned England large sums of money. In fact, J. P. Morgan & Co. served as British financial agents in this country during World War I.

While all of the standard reasons given for the outbreak of World War I in Europe doubtless were factors, there were also other more important causes. The conspiracy had been planning the war for over two decades.

The assassination of an Austrian Archduke was merely an incident providing an excuse for starting a chain reaction.

After years of fighting, the war was a complete stalemate and would have ended almost immediately in a negotiated settlement (as had most other European conflicts) had not the U. S. declared war on Germany.

As soon as Wilson's re-election had been engineered through the "he kept us out of war" slogan, a complete reversal of propaganda was instituted. In those days before radio and television, public opinion was controlled almost exclusively by newspapers. Many of the major newspapers were controlled by the Federal Reserve crowd. Now they began beating the drums over the "inevitability of war." Arthur Ponsonby, a member of the British parliament, admitted in his book *Falsehood In War Time* (E. P. Dutton & Co., Inc., New York, 1928): "There must have been more deliberate lying in the world from 1914 to 1918 than in any other period of the world's history." Propaganda concerning the war was heavily one-sided. Although after the war many historians admitted that one side was as guilty as the other in starting the war, Germany was pictured as a militaristic monster which wanted to rule the world. Remember, this picture was painted by Britain which had its soldiers in more countries around the world than all other nations put together. So-called "Prussian militarism" did exist, but it was no threat to conquer the world. Meanwhile, the sun never set on the British Empire! Actually, the Germans were proving to be tough business competitors in the world's markets and the British did not approve.

In order to generate war fever, the sinking of the Lusitania—a British ship torpedoed two years earlier—was revived and given renewed headlines. German submarine warfare was turned into a major issue by the newspapers.

Submarine warfare was a phony issue. Germany and England were at war. Each was blockading the other country. J. P. Morgan and other financiers were selling munitions to Britain. The Germans could not allow those supplies to be delivered any more than the English would have allowed them to be delivered to Germany. If Morgan wanted to take the risks and reap the rewards (or suffer the consequences) of selling munitions to England, that was his business. It was certainly nothing over which the entire nation should have been dragged into war.

The Lusitania, at the time it was sunk, was carrying six million pounds of ammunition. It was actually illegal for American passengers to be aboard a ship carrying munitions to belligerents. Almost two years before the liner was sunk, the *New York Tribune* (June 19, 1913) carried a squib which stated: "Cunard officials acknowledged to the *Tribune* correspondent today that the greyhound [Lusitania] is being equipped with high power naval rifles. . . ." In fact, the Lusitania was registered in the British navy as an auxiliary cruiser. (Barnes, Harry E., *The Genesis of the War,* Alfred Knopf, New York, 1926, p. 611.) In addition, the German government took out large ads in all the New York papers warning potential passengers that the ship was carrying munitions and telling them not to cross the Atlantic on it. Those who chose to make the trip knew the risk they were taking. Yet the sinking of the Lusitania was used by clever propagandists to portray the Germans as inhuman slaughterers of innocents. Submarine warfare was manufactured into a *cause celebre* to push us into war. On April 6, 1917, Congress declared war. The American people acquiesced on the basis that it would be a "war to end all wars."

During the "war to end all wars," *Insider* banker Bernard Baruch was made absolute dictator over American business when President Wilson appointed him Chairman of the War Industries Board, where he had control of all domestic contracts for Allied war materials. Baruch made lots of friends while placing tens of billions in government contracts, and it was widely rumored in Wall Street that out of the war to make the world safe for international bankers he netted $200 million for himself.

"Colonel" House (l) was front man for the international banking fraternity. He manipulated President Woodrow Wilson (r) like a puppet. Wilson called him "my alter ego." House played a major role in creating the Federal Reserve System, passing the graduated income tax and getting America into WWI. House's influence over Wilson is an example that in the world of super-politics the real rulers are not always the ones the public sees.

German born international financier Paul Warburg masterminded establishment of Federal Reserve to put control over nation's economy in hands of international bankers. The Federal Reserve controls the money supply which allows manipulators to create alternate cycles of boom and bust, i.e., a roller coaster economy. This allows those in the know to make fabulous amounts of money, but even more important, allows the **Insiders** to control the economy and further centralize power in the federal government.

While *Insider* banker Paul Warburg controlled the Federal Reserve, and international banker Bernard Baruch placed government contracts, international banker Eugene Meyer, a former partner of Baruch and the son of a partner in the Rothschilds' international banking house of Lazard Freres, was Wilson's choice to head the War Finance Corporation, where he too made a little money.*

It should be noted that Sir William Wiseman, the man sent by British Intelligence to help bring the United States into the war, was amply rewarded for his services. He stayed in this country after WWI as a new partner in the Jacob Schiff-Paul Warburg-controlled Kuhn, Loeb bank.

World War I was a financial bonanza for the international bankers. But it was a catastrophe of such magnitude for the United States that few even today grasp its importance. The war reversed our traditional foreign policy of non-involvement and we have been enmeshed almost constantly ever since in perpetual wars for perpetual peace. Winston Churchill once observed that all nations would have been better off had the U. S. minded its own buisness. Had we done so, he said, "peace would have been made with Germany; and there would have been no collapse in Russia leading to Communism; no breakdown of government in Italy followed by Fascism; and Naziism never would have gained ascendancy in Germany." *(Social Justice* Magazine, July 3, 1939, p. 4.)

The Bolshevik Revolution in Russia was obviously one of the great turning points in world history. It is an event over which misinformation abounds. The myth-makers and re-writers of history have done their landscape painting jobs well. The establishing of Communism in Russia is a classic example of the second "big lie" of Communism, i.e., that it is the movement of the downtrodden masses rising up against exploiting bosses. This cunning decep-

(*Meyer later gained control of the highly influential *Washington Post* which became known as the "*Washington Daily Worker.*")

66

tion has been fostered since before the first French Revolution in 1789.

Most people today believe the Communists were successful in Russia because they were able to rally behind them the sympathy and frustration of the Russian people who were sick of the tyranny of the Czars. This is to ignore the history of what actually happened. While almost everybody is reminded that the Bolshevik Revolution took place in November of 1917, few know that the Czar had abdicated seven months earlier in March. When Czar Nicholas II abdicated, a provisional government was established by Prince Lvov who wanted to pattern the new Russian government after our own. But, unfortunately, the Lvov government gave way to the Kerensky regime. Kerensky, a so-called democratic socialist, may have been running a caretaker government for the Communists. He kept the war going against Germany and the other Central Powers, but he issued a general amnesty for Communists and other revolutionaries, many of whom had been exiled after the abortive Red Revolution of 1905. Back to mother Russia came 250,000 dedicated revolutionaries, and Kerensky's own government's doom was sealed.

In the Soviet Union, as in every Communist country (or as they call themselves—the Socialist countries), the power has not come to the Communists' hands because the downtrodden masses willed it so. The power has come *from the top down* in every instance. Let us briefly reconstruct the sequence of the Communist takeover.

The year is 1917. The Allies are fighting the Central Powers. The Allies include Russia, the British Commonwealth, France and by April 1917, the United States. In March of 1917, purposeful planners set in motion the forces to compel Czar Nicholas II to abdicate. He did so under pressure from the Allies after severe riots in the Czarist capitol of Petrograd, riots that were caused by the breakdowns in the transportation system which cut the city off from food supplies and led to the closing of factories.

But where were Lenin and Trotsky when all this was taking place? Lenin was in Switzerland and had been in Western Europe since 1905 when he was exiled for trying to topple the Czar in the abortive Communist revolution of that year. Trotsky also was in exile, a reporter for a Communist newspaper on the lower east side of New York City. The Bolsheviks were not a viable political force at the time the Czar abdicated. And they came to power not because the donwtrodden masses of Russia called them *back,* but because very powerful men in Europe and the United States *sent them in.*

Lenin was sent across Europe-at-war on the famous "sealed train." With him Lenin took some $5 to $6 million in gold. The whole thing was arranged by the German high command and Max Warburg, through another very wealthy and life-long socialist by the name of Alexander Helphand alias "Parvus." When Trotsky left New York aboard the S. S. Christiania, on March 27, 1917, with his entourage of 275 revolutionaries, the first port of call was Halifax, Nova Scotia. There the Canadians grabbed Trotsky and his money and impounded them both. This was a very logical thing for the Canadian government to do for Trotsky had said many times that if he were successful in coming to power in Russia he would immediately stop what he called the "imperialist war" and sue for a separate peace with Germany. This would free millions of German troops for transfer from the Eastern front to the Western front where they could kill Canadians. So Trotsky cooled his heels in a Canadian prison—for five days. Then all of a sudden the British (through future Kuhn, Loeb partner Sir William Wiseman) and the United States (through none other than the ubiquitous "Colonel" House) pressured the Canadian government. And, despite the fact we were now in the war, said, in so many words, "Let Trotsky go." Thus, with an American passport, Trotsky went back to meet Lenin. They joined up, and, by November, through bribery, cunning, brutality and deception, they were able (not to bring the masses rallying to their cause, but) to hire enough thugs and make enough deals to impose out of the gun barrel what Lenin called "all power to the Soviets." The Communists came to power by seizing a mere handful of key cities. In fact, practically the whole Bolshevik Revolution took place in one city—Petrograd. It was as if the whole United States became Communist because a Communist-led mob seized Washington, D. C. It was years before the Soviets solidified power throughout Russia.

The Germans, on the face of it, had a plausible excuse for financing Lenin and Trotsky. The two Germans most responsible for the financing of Lenin were Max Warburg and a displaced Russian named Alexander Helphand. They could claim that they were serving their country's cause by helping and financing Lenin. However, these two German "patriots" neglected to mention to the Kaiser their plan to foment a Communist revolution in Russia. The picture takes on another dimension when you consider that the brother of Max Warburg was Paul Warburg, prime mover in establishing the Federal Reserve System and who from his position on the Federal Reserve Board of Directors, played a key role in financing the American war effort. (When news leaked out in American papers about brother Max running the German finances, Paul resigned from his Federal Reserve post without a whimper.) From here on the plot sickens.

For the father-in-law of Max Warburg's brother, Felix, was Jacob Schiff, senior partner in Kuhn, Loeb & Co. (Paul and Felix Warburg, you will recall, were also partners in Kuhn, Loeb & Co. while Max ran the Rothschild-allied family bank of Frankfurt.) Jacob Schiff also helped finance Leon Trotsky. According to the *New York Journal-American* of February 3, 1949: "Today it is estimated by Jacob's grandson, John Schiff, that the old man sank about 20,000,000 dollars for the final triumph of Bolshevism in Russia." (See Chart 6.)

One of the best sources of information on the financing of the Bolshevik Revolution is *Czarism and the Revolu-*

tion by an important White Russian General named Arsene de Goulevitch who was founder in France of the Union of Oppressed Peoples. In this volume, written in French and subsequently translated into English, de Goulevitch notes:

"The main purveyors of funds for the revolution, however, were neither the crackpot Russian millionaires nor the armed bandits of Lenin. The 'real' money primarily came from certain British and American circles which for a long time past had lent their support to the Russian revolutionary cause. . . ."

de Goulevitch continues:

"The important part played by the wealthy American banker, Jacob Schiff, in the events in Russia, though as yet only partially revealed, is no longer a secret."

General Alexander Nechvolodov is quoted by de Goulevitch as stating in his book on the Bolshevik Revolution:

"In April 1917, Jacob Schiff publicly declared that it was thanks to his financial support that the revolution in Russia had succeeded.

In the Spring of the same year, Schiff commenced to subsidize Trotsky . . .

Simultaneously Trotsky and Co. were also being subsidized by Max Warburg and Olaf Aschberg of the Nye Banken of Stockholm . . . the Rhine Westphalian Syndicate and Jivotovsky, . . . whose daughter later married Trotsky."

Chart 6

FINANCING
BOLSHEVIK REVOLUTION

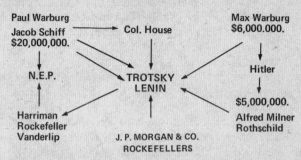

Schiff spent millions to overthrow the Czar and more millions to overthrow Kerensky. He was sending money to Russia long after the true character of the Bolsheviks was known to the world. Schiff raised $10 million, supposedly for Jewish war relief in Russia, but later events revealed it to be a good business investment. (Forbes, B. C., *Men Who Are Making America,* pp. 334-5.)

According to de Goulevitch:

> "Mr. Bakhmetiev, the late Russian Imperial Ambassador to the United States, tells us that the Bolsheviks, after victory, transferred 600 million roubles in gold between the years 1918 and 1922 to Kuhn, Loeb & Company [Schiff's firm]."

Schiff's participation in the Bolshevik Revolution, though quite naturally now denied, was well known among Allied intelligence services at the time. This led to much talk about Bolshevism being a Jewish plot. The result was that the subject of financing the Communist takeover of Russia became taboo. Later evidence indicates that the bankrolling of the Bolsheviks was handled by a syndicate of international bankers, which in addition to the Schiff-Warburg clique, included Morgan and Rockefeller interests. Documents show that the Morgan organization put at least $1 million in the Red revolutionary kitty.*

Still another important financier of the Bolshevik Revolution was an extremely wealthy Englishman named Lord Alfred Milner, the organizer and head of a secret organization called "The Round Table" Group which was backed by Lord Rothschild (discussed in the next chapter).

De Goulevitch notes further:

"On April 7, 1917, General Janin made the following entry in his diary ('Au G.C.C. Russé'—At Russian G.H.Q.—Le Monde Slave, Vol. 2, 1927, pp. 296-297): Long interview with R., who confirmed what I had previously been told by M. After referring to the German hatred of himself and his family, he turned to the subject of the Revolution which, he claimed, was engineered by the English and, more precisely, by Sir George Buchanan and Lord [Alfred] Milner. Petrograd at the time was teeming with English. . . . He could, he asserted, name the streets and the numbers of the houses in which British agents were quartered. They were reported, during the rising, to have distributed money to the soldiers and incited them to mutiny."

De Goulevitch goes on to reveal: "In private interviews I have been told that over 21 million roubles were spent by Lord Milner in financing the Russian Revolution."

It should be noted parenthetically that Lord Milner, Paul, Felix and Max Warburg represented "their" respective countries at the Paris Peace Conference at the conclusion of World War I.

If we can somehow ascribe Max Warburg's financing of Lenin to German "patriotism," it was certainly not "patriotism" which inspired Schiff, Morgan, Rockefeller and Milner to bankroll the Bolsheviks. Both Britain and

(*Hagedorn, Herman, *The Magnate,* John Day, N.Y. See also *Washington Post,* Feb. 2, 1918, p. 195.)

America were at war with Germany and were allies of Czarist Russia. To free dozens of German divisions to switch from the Eastern front to France and kill hundreds of thousands of American and British soldiers was nothing short of treason.

In the Bolshevik Revolution we see many of the same old faces that were responsible for creating the Federal Reserve System, initiating the graduated income tax, setting up the tax-free foundations and pushing us into WWI. However, if you conclude that this is anything but coincidental, your name will be immediately expunged from the Social Register.

No revolution can be successful without organization and money. "The downtrodden masses" usually provide little of the former and none of the latter. But *Insiders* at the top can arrange for both.

What did these people possibly have to gain in financing the Russian Revolution? What did they have to gain by keeping it alive and afloat, or, during the 1920's by pouring millions of dollars into what Lenin called his New Economic Program, thus saving the Soviets from collapse?

Why would these "capitalists" do all this? If your goal is global conquest, you have to start somewhere. It may or may not have been coincidental, but Russia was the one major European country without a central bank. In Russia, for the first time, the Communist conspiracy gained a geographical homeland from which to launch assaults against the other nations of the world. The West now had an enemy.

In the Bolshevik Revolution we have some of the world's richest and most powerful men financing a movement which claims its very existence is based on the concept of stripping of their wealth men like the Rothschilds, Rockefellers, Schiffs, Warburgs, Morgans, Harrimans, and Milners. But obviously these men have no fear of international Communism. It is only logical to assume that if they financed it and do not fear it, it must be because they control it. Can there be any other explanation that makes sense? Remember that for over 150 years it has been

Lord Alfred Milner, wealthy Englishman and front man for the Rothschilds, served as paymaster for the international bankers in Petrograd during the Bolshevik Revolution. Milner later headed secret society known as The Round Table which was dedicated to establishing a world government whereby a clique of super-rich financiers would control the world under the guise of Socialism. The American subsidiary of this conspiracy is called the Council on Foreign Relations and was started by, and is still controlled by Leftist international bankers.

According to his grandson John, Jacob Schiff (above), long-time associate of the Rothschilds, financed the Communist Revolution in Russia to the tune of $20 million. According to a report on file with the State Department, his firm, Kuhn Loeb and Co. bankrolled the first five year plan for Stalin. Schiff's partner and relative, Paul Warburg, engineered the establishment of the Federal Reserve System while on the Kuhn Loeb payroll. Schiff's descendants are active in the Council on Foreign Relations today.

Home of the Council on Foreign Relations on 68th St. in New York. The admitted goal of the CFR is to abolish the Constitution and replace our once independent Republic with a World Government. CFR members have controlled the last six administrations. Richard Nixon has been a member and has appointed at least 100 CFR members to high positions in his administration.

standard operating procedure of the Rothschilds and their allies to control both sides of every conflict. You must have an "enemy" if you are going to collect from the King. The East-West balance-of-power politics is used as one of the main excuses for the socialization of America. Although it was not their main purpose, by nationalization of Russia the *Insiders* bought themselves an enormous piece of real estate, complete with mineral rights, for somewhere between $30 and $40 million.

We can only theorize on the manner in which Moscow is controlled from New York, London and Paris. Undoubtedly much of the control is economic, but certainly the international bankers have an enforcer arm within Russia to keep the Soviet leaders in line. The organization may be SMERSH, the international Communist murder organization described in testimony before Congressional Committees and by Ian Fleming in his James Bond books. For although the Bond novels were wildly imaginative, Fleming had been in British Navy intelligence, maintained excellent intelligence contacts around the world and was reputedly a keen student of the international conspiracy.

We do know this, however. A clique of American financiers not only helped establish Communism in Russia, but has striven mightily ever since to keep it alive. Ever since 1918 this clique has been engaged in transferring money and, probably more important, technical information, to the Soviet Union. This is made abundantly clear in the three volume history *Western Technology and Soviet Economic Development* by scholar Antony Sutton of Stanford University's Hoover Institution on War, Revolution and Peace. Using, for the most part, official State Department documents, Sutton shows conclusively that virtually everything the Soviets possess has been acquired from the West. It is not much of an exaggeration to say that the U.S.S.R. was made in the U.S.A.. The landscape painters, unable to refute Sutton's monumental scholarship, simply paint him out of the picture.

At Versailles, this same clique carved up Europe and

set the stage for World War II. As Lord Curzon commented: "It is not a peace treaty, it is simply a break in hostilities." In 1933, the same *Insiders* pushed FDR into recognizing the Soviet Union, thus saving it from financial collapse, while at the same time they were underwriting huge loans on both sides of the Atlantic for the new regime of Adolph Hitler. In so doing they assisted greatly in setting the stage for World War II, and the events that followed. In 1941, the same *Insiders* rushed to the aid of our "noble ally," Stalin, after his break with Hitler. In 1943, these same *Insiders* marched off to the Teheran Conference and proceeded to start the carving up of Europe after the second great "war to end war." Again at Yalta and Potsdam in 1945, they established the China policy . . . later summarized by Owen Lattimore: "The problem was how to allow them [China] to fall without making it look as if the United States had pushed them." The facts are inescapable. In one country after another Communism has been imposed on the local population from the top down. The most prominent forces for the imposition of that tyranny came from the United States and Great Britian. Here is a charge that no American enjoys making, but the facts lead to no other possible conclusion. The idea that Communism is a movement of the downtrodden masses is a fraud.

None of the foregoing makes sense if Communism really is what the Communists and the Establishment tell us it is. But if Communism is an arm of a bigger conspiracy to control the world by power-mad billionaires (and brilliant but ruthless academicians who have shown them how to use their power) it all becomes perfectly logical.

It is at this point that we should again make it clear that this conspiracy is not made up solely of bankers and international cartelists, but includes every field of human endeavor. Starting with Voltaire and Adam Weishaupt and running through John Ruskin, Sidney Webb, Nicholas Murray Butler, and on to the present with Henry Kissinger and John Kenneth Galbraith, it has always been the scholar looking for avenues of power who has shown the "sons of the very powerful" how their wealth could be used to rule the world.

We cannot stress too greatly the importance of the reader keeping in mind that this book is discussing only one segment of the conspiracy, certain international bankers. Other equally important segments which work to foment labor, religious and racial strife in order to promote socialism have been described in numerous other books. These other divisions of the conspiracy operate independently of the international bankers in most cases and it would certainly be disastrous to ignore the danger to our freedom they represent.

It would be equally disastrous to lump all businessmen and bankers into the conspiracy. One must draw the distinction between competitive free enterprise, the most moral and productive system ever devised, and cartel capitalism dominated by industrial monopolists and international bankers. The difference is the private enterpriser operates by offering products and services in a competitive free market while the cartel capitalist uses the government to force the public to do business with him. These corporate socialists are the deadly enemies of competitive private enterprise.

Liberals are willing to believe that these "robber barons" will fix prices, rig markets, establish monopolies, buy politicians, exploit employees and fire them the day before they are eligible for pensions, but they absolutely will not believe that these same men would want to rule the world or would use Communism as the striking edge of their conspiracy. When one discusses the machinations of these men, Liberals usually respond by saying, "But don't you think they mean well?"

However, if you think with logic, reason and precision in this field and try to expose these power seekers, the Establishment's mass media will accuse you of being a dangerous paranoid who is "dividing" our people. In every other area, of course, they encourage dissent as being healthy in a "democracy."

CHAPTER FIVE

ESTABLISHING THE ESTABLISHMENT

One of the primary reasons the *Insiders* worked behind the scenes to foment WWI was to create in its aftermath a world government. If you wish to establish national monopolies, you must control national governments. If you wish to establish international monopolies or cartels, you must control a world government.

After the Armistice on November 11, 1918, Woodrow Wilson and his *alter ego,* "Colonel" House (the ever present front man for the *Insiders*), went to Europe in hopes of establishing a world government in the form of the League of Nations. When the negotiations revealed one side had been about as guilty as the other, and the glitter of the "moral crusade" evaporated along with Wilson's vaunted "Fourteen Points," the "rubes back on Main Street" began to waken. Reaction and disillusionment set in.

Americans certainly didn't want to get into a World Government with double-dealing Europeans whose specialty was secret treaty hidden behind secret treaty. The guest of honor, so to speak, stalked out of the banquet before the poisoned meal could be served. And, without American inclusion, there could be no meaningful World Government.

Aroused public opinion made it obvious that the U. S. Senate dared not ratify a treaty saddling the country with such an internationalist commitment. In some manner the American public had to be sold on the idea of internationalism and World Government. Again, the key was "Colonel" House.

House had set down his political ideas in his book called *Philip Dru: Administrator* in 1912. In this book House laid out a thinly fictionalized plan for conquest of America by establishing "Socialism as dreamed by Karl Marx." He described a "conspiracy"—the word is his—which succeeds in electing a U. S. President by means of "deception regarding his real opinions and intentions." Among other things, House wrote that the conspiracy was to insinuate "itself into the primaries, in order that no candidate might be nominated whose views were not in accord with theirs." Elections were to become mere charades conducted for the bedazzlement of the booboisie. The idea was to use both the Democrat and Republican parties as instruments to promote World Government.

In 1919 House met in Paris with members of a British "secret society" called The Round Table in order to form an organization whose job it would be to propagandize the citizens of America, England and Western Europe on the glories of World Government. The big selling point, of course, was "peace." The part about the *Insiders* establishing a world dictatorship quite naturally was left out.

The Round Table organization in England grew out of the life-long dream of gold and diamond magnate Cecil Rhodes for a "new world order."

Rhodes' biographer Sara Millin was a little more direct. As she put it: "The government of the world was Rhodes' simple desire." Quigley notes:

"In the middle 1890's Rhodes had a personal income of at least a million pounds sterling a year (then about five million dollars) which he spent so freely for his mysterious purposes that he was usually overdrawn on his account. . . ."

Cecil Rhodes' commitment to a conspiracy to establish World Government was set down in a series of wills described by Frank Aydelotte in his book *American Rhodes Scholarships*. Aydelotte writes:

"The seven wills which Cecil Rhodes made between the ages of 24 and 46 [Rhodes died at age forty-eight] constitute a kind of spiritual autobiography. . . . Best known are the first (the Secret Society Will . . .), and the last, which established the Rhodes Scholarships. . . .

In his first will Rhodes states his aim still more specifically: 'The extension of British rule throughout the world. . . . the foundation of so great a power as to hereafter render wars impossible and promote the interests of humanity.'

The 'Confession of Faith' enlarges upon these ideas. The model for this proposed secret society was the Society of Jesus, though he mentions also the Masons."

It should be noted that the originator of this type of secret society was Adam Weishaupt, the monster who founded the Order of Illuminati on May 1, 1776, for the purpose of conspiracy to control the world. The role of Weishaupt's Illuminists in such horrors as the Reign of Terror is unquestioned, and the techniques of the Illuminati have long been recognized as models for Communist methodology. Weishaupt also used the structure of the Society of Jesus (the Jesuits) as his model, and rewrote his Code in Masonic terms. Aydelotte continues:

"In 1888 Rhodes made his third will . . . leaving everything to Lord Rothschild [his financier in mining enterprises], with an accompanying letter enclosing 'the written matter discussed between us.' This, one surmises, consisted of the first will and the 'Confession of Faith,' since in a postscript Rhodes says 'in considering questions suggested take Constitution of the Jesuits if obtainable. . . .' "

Apparently for strategic reasons Lord Rothschild was subsequently removed from the forefront of the scheme. Professor Quigley reveals that Lord Rosebury "replaced his father-in-law, Lord Rothschild, in Rhodes' secret group and was made a Trustee under Rhodes' next (and last), will."

The "secret society" was organized on the conspiratorial

80

pattern of circles within circles. Professor Quigley informs us that the central part of the "secret society" was established by March, 1891, using Rhodes' money. The organization was run for Rothschild by Lord Alfred Milner, discussed in the last chapter as a key financier of the Bolshevik revolution. The Round Table worked behind the scenes at the highest levels of British government, influencing foreign policy and England's involvement and conduct of WWI. According to Professor Quigley:

"At the end of the war of 1914, it became clear that the organization of this system [the Round Table Group] had to be greatly extended. Once again the task was entrusted to Lionel Curtis who established, in England and each dominion, a front organization to the existing Round Table Group. This front organization, called the Royal Institute of International Affairs, had as its nucleus in each area the existing submerged Round Table Group. In New York it was known as the Council on Foreign Relations, and was a front for J. P. Morgan and Company in association with the very small American Round Table Group. The American organizers were dominated by the large number of Morgan 'experts,' . . . who had gone to the Paris Peace Conference and there became close friends with the similar group of English 'experts' which had been recruited by the Milner group. In fact, the original plans for the Royal Institute of International Affairs and the Council on Foreign Relations [C.F.R.] were drawn up in Paris. . . ."

Joseph Kraft (C.F.R.), however, tells us in *Harper's* of July 1958, that the chief agent in the formal founding of the Council on Foreign Relations was "Colonel" House, *supported* by such protegés as Walter Lippmann, John Foster Dulles, Allen Dulles and Christian Herter. It was House who acted as host for the Round Table Group, both English and American, at the key meeting of May 19,

1919, in the Majestic Hotel, Paris, which committed the conspiracy to creation of the C.F.R.

Although Quigley stresses the importance of Morgan men at the creation of the organization known as the Council on Foreign Relations, this organization's own materials and "Colonel" House's own memoirs reveal his function as midwife at the birth of the C.F.R.

The C.F.R.'s Twenty-Fifth Annual Report tells us this of the C.F.R.'s founding at Paris:

> ". . . The Institute of International Affairs founded at Paris in 1919 was comprised, at the outset, of two branches, one in the United Kingdom and one in the U.S. . . ."

Later the plan was changed to create an ostensible autonomy because, ". . . it seemed unwise to set up a single institute with branches." It had to be made to appear that the C.F.R. in America, and the R.I.I.A in Britain, were really independent bodies, lest the American public become aware the C.F.R. was in fact a subsidiary of the Round Table Group and react in patriotic fury.

According to Quigley, the most important financial dynasties in America following WWI were (in addition to Morgan) the Rockefeller family; Kuhn, Loeb & Company; Dillon Read and Company and Brown Bros. Harriman. All were represented in the C.F.R. and Paul Warburg was one of the incorporators. The *Insider* crowd which created the Federal Reserve System, many of whom also bankrolled the Bolshevik Revolution, were all in the original membership. In addition to Paul Warburg, founders of the C.F.R. included international financial *Insiders* Jacob Schiff, Averell Harriman, Frank Vanderlip, Nelson Aldrich, Bernard Baruch, J. P. Morgan and John D. Rockefeller. These men did not create the C.F.R. because they had nothing better to do with their time and money. They created it as a tool to further their ambitions.

The C.F.R. has come to be known as "The Establishment," "the invisible government" and "the Rockefeller foreign office." This semi-secret organization unquestionably has become the most influential group in America.

One of the extremely infrequent articles to appear in the national press concerning this Council was published in the *Christian Science Monitor* of September 1, 1961. It began this way:

> "On the west side of fashionable Park Avenue at 68th Street [in New York City] sit two handsome buildings across the way from each other. One is the Soviet Embassy to the United Nations. . . . Directly opposite on the southwest corner is the Council on Foreign Relations—probably one of the most influential semi-public organizations in the field of foreign policy."

Although the formal membership in the C.F.R. is composed of close to 1500 of the most elite names in the worlds of government, labor, business, finance, communications, the foundations, and the academy—and despite the fact that it has staffed almost every key position of every administration since those of FDR—it is doubtful that one American in a thousand so much as recognizes the Council's name, or that one in ten thousand can relate anything at all about its structure or purpose. Indicative of the C.F.R.'s power to maintain its anonymity is the fact that, despite its having been operative at the highest levels for nearly fifty years and having from the beginning counted among its members the foremost lions of the Establishment communications media, we discovered after poring over volumnes of the *Readers' Guide To Periodical Literature* covering several decades that only one magazine article on the C.F.R. has ever appeared in a major national journal—and that in *Harper's,* hardly a mass-circulation periodical. Similarly, only a handful of articles on the Council have appeared in the nation's great newspapers. Such anonymity—at that level—can hardly be a matter of mere chance.

What makes this secret organization so influential? No one who knows for a certainty will say. The *Christian Science Monitor,* which is edited by a member of the American Round Table (a branch of Milner's secret society) did note in the article of September 1, 1961, that "Its roster . . . contains names distinguished in the field of diplomacy, government, business, finance, science, labor, journalism, law and education. What united so wide-ranging and disparate a membership is a passionate concern for the direction of American foreign policy."

The *Christian Science Monitor* indicates the fantastic power the C.F.R. has had during the last six administrations:

> "Because of the Council's single-minded dedication to studying and deliberating American foreign policy, there is a constant flow of its members from private to public service. *Almost half of the Council members have been invited to assume official government positions or to act as consultants at one time or another.*" [Emphasis added]

The policies promoted by the C.F.R. in the fields of defense and international relations become, with a regularity which defies the laws of chance, the official policies of the United States Government. As Liberal columnist Joseph Kraft, himself a member of the C.F.R., noted of the Council in the *Harper's* article: "It has been the seat of some basic government decisions, has set the context for many more, and has repeatedly served as a recruiting ground for ranking officials." Kraft, incidentally, aptly titled his article on the C.F.R., "School for Statesmen"—an admission that the members of the Council are drilled with a "line" of strategy to be carried out in Washington.

As World War II approached, the Round Table Group was influential in seeing that Hitler was not stopped in Austria, the Rhineland, or Sudetenland—and thereby was largely responsible for precipitating the holocaust. A second world war would greatly enhance the opportunity for establishment of World Government. The financing for Adolph Hitler's rise to power was handled through the Warburg-controlled Mendelsohn Bank of Amsterdam and later by the J. Henry Schroeder Bank with branches in Frankfurt, London and New York. Chief legal counsel to the J. Henry Schroeder Bank was the firm of Sullivan and Cromwell whose senior partners included John Foster and Allen Dulles, (See James Martin's *All Honorable Men*, Little Brown Co., New York, 1950, p 51. See also Quigley, p. 433.)

With the Round Table doing its work in Europe, the C.F.R. carried the ball in the United States. The Council's first task was to infiltrate and develop effective control of the U.S. State Department—to make certain that after World War II there would be no slip-ups as there had been following World War I. The story of the C.F.R. takeover of the Department of State is contained in State Department Publication 2349, *Report To The President On The Results of the San Francisco Conference*. It is the report of Secretary of State Edward R. Stettinius (C.F.R.) to President Truman. On page twenty we find:

"With the outbreak of war in Europe it was clear that the United States would be confronted, after the war, with new and exceptional problems. . . . Accordingly, a Committee on Post-War Problems was set up before the end of 1939 [two years before the U. S. entered the war], at the suggestion of the C.F.R. The Committee consisted of high officials of the Department of State [all but one of whom were C.F.R. members]. It was assisted by a research staff [provided by, financed by, and directed by the C.F.R.], which in February, 1941, was organized into a Division of Special Research [and went off the C.F.R. payroll and onto that of the State Department].

[After Pearl Harbor] the research facilities were rapidly expanded, and the Departmental Committee on Post-War Problems was reorganized into an Advisory Committee on Post-War Foreign Policies [completely staffed by the C.F.R.]." (See also the C.F.R.'s booklet, *A Record of Twenty Years, 1921-1947.)*

This is the group which designed the United Nations—the first major successful step on the road to a World Superstate. At least forty-seven C.F.R. members were among the American delegates to the founding of the United Nations in San Francisco in 1945. Members of the C.F.R. group included Harold Stassen, John J. McCloy, Owen Lattimore (called by the Senate Internal Security Subcommittee a "conscious articulate instrument of the Soviet conspiracy"), Alger Hiss(Communist spy), Philip Jessup, Harry Dexter White (Communist agent), Nelson Rockefeller, John Foster Dulles, John Carter Vincent (security risk), and Dean Acheson. Just to make sure that Communist Party members understood the importance of the U.N. establishment, *Political Affairs,* the Party's official theoretical journal, in the April 1945 issue, gave the order:

> "Great popular support and enthusiasm for the United Nations policies should be built up, well organized and fully articulate. But it is also necessary to do more than that. The opposition must be rendered so impotent that it will be unable to gather any significant support in the Senate against the United Nations Charter and the treaties which will follow."

One wonders if the boobs at the Party level ever questioned why they were to support an organization dominated by the hated "Wall Street" personalities. The landscape painters of the mass media have outdone themselves painting the U. N. as a peace organization instead of a front for the international bankers.

Not only did members of the Council on Foreign Relations dominate the establishment of the U.N., but C.F.R.

members were at the elbow of the American President at Teheran, Potsdam and Yalta—where hundreds of millions of human beings were delivered into the hands of Joseph Stalin, vastly extending the power of the International Communist Conspiracy. Administrative assistant to FDR during this time was a key member of the C.F.R. named Lauchlin Currie—subsequently identified by J. Edgar Hoover as a Soviet agent.

So completely has the C.F.R. dominated the State Department over the past thirty-eight years that every Secretary of State except Cordell Hull, James Byrnes, and William Rogers has been a member of the C.F.R. While Rogers is not a member, Professor Henry Kissinger, Mr. Nixon's chief foreign policy advisor, came to the job from the staff of the C.F.R., and the undersecretaries of state, almost to a man, are C.F.R. members.

Today the C.F.R. remains active in working toward its final goal of a government over all the world—a government which the *Insiders* and their allies will control. The goal of the C.F.R. is simply to abolish the United States with its Constitutional guarantees of liberty. And they don't even try to hide it. *Study No. 7,* published by the C.F.R. on November 25, 1959, openly advocates "building a new international order [which] must be responsive to world aspirations for peace, [and] for social and economic change . . . an international order [code word for world government] . . . including states labeling themselves as 'Socialist' [Communist]."

The reason is evident to those who have studied its membership for this little known semi-secret organization to be called "the Establishment." (See Chart 7) International banking organizations that currently have men in the C.F.R. include Kuhn, Loeb & Company; Lazard Freres (directly affiliated with Rothschild); Dillon Read; Lehman Bros.; Goldman, Sachs; Chase Manhattan Bank; Morgan Guaranty Bank; Brown Bros. Harriman; First National City Bank; Chemical Bank & Trust, and Manufacturers Hanover Trust Bank.

Among the major corporations that have men in the

Chart 7

WORLD SUPRA-GOVERNMENT

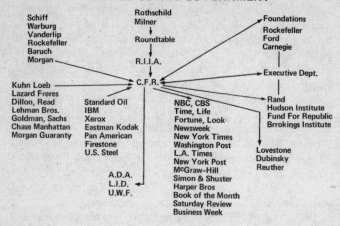

C.F.R. are Standard Oil, IBM, Xerox, Eastman Kodak, Pan American, Firestone, U. S. Steel, General Electric and American Telephone and Telegraph Company.

Also in the C.F.R. are men from such openly Leftist organizations as the Fabian Socialist Americans for Democratic Action, the avowedly Socialist League for Industrial Democracy—(formerly the Intercollegiate Socialist Society), and the United World Federalists which openly advocates world government with the Communists. Such devotedly Socialist labor leaders as the late Walter Reuther, David Dubinsky and Jay Lovestone have also been members of the C.F.R. In theory, these men and organizations are supposed to be the blood enemies of the banks and businesses listed above. Yet they all belong to the same lodge. You can see why that fact is not advertised.

The C.F.R. is totally interlocked with the major foundations and so-called "Think Tanks." Included in the interlock are the Rockefeller, Ford and Carnegie foundations and the Rand Corporation, Hudson Institute, Fund for the Republic and Brookings Institute "Think Tanks."

The fact that the C.F.R. operates in near-complete anonymity can hardly be accidental. Among the communications corporations represented in the C.F.R. are National Broadcasting Corporation, Columbia Broadcasting System, *Time, Life, Fortune, Look, Newsweek, New York Times, Washington Post, Los Angeles Times, New York Post, Denver Post, Louisville Courier Journal, Minneapolis Tribune,* the Knight papers, McGraw-Hill, Simon & Shuster, Harper Bros., Random House, Little Brown & Co., Macmillan Co., Viking Press, *Saturday Review, Business Week* and Book of the Month Club. Surely the C.F.R. could get a few blurbs of publicity if publicity were desired. If it seems impossible that one entity could control such a vast array of firms, it is because most people do not know that the so-called founders of such giants as the *New York Times* and NBC were chosen, financed and directed by Morgan, Schiff and their allies. The case of Adolph Ochs of the *Times* and David Sarnoff of RCA are examples of this control. Both were given early financial aid by Kuhn, Loeb & Company and Morgan Guaranty.

These are the Establishment's official landscape painters whose jobs it is to make sure the public does not discover the C.F.R. and its role in creating a world socialist dictatorship.

You will recall that "Colonel" House believed we should have two political parties but only a single ideology— One World socialism. This is exactly what we have in this country today. (See Chart 8) Although there are philosophical differences between the grass roots Democrats and the grass roots Republicans, yet as you move up the party ladders these differences become less and less distinguishable until finally the ladders disappear behind the Establishment's managed news curtain and come together at the apex under the control of the C.F.R. In 1968, when George Wallace maintained that there wasn't a dime's worth of difference between the two parties, he may not have known how right he was or why.

Chart 8

CONTROL OF POLITICAL PARTIES

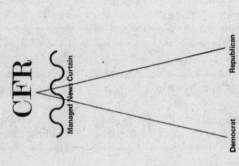

Democrats
Dean Acheson
Alger Hiss
Adlai Stevenson
John Kennedy
Edward Kennedy
Robert Kennedy
Averell Harriman
George Ball
Henry Fowler
Dean Rusk
Adam Yarmolinsky
John K. Galbraith
Arthur Schlesinger, Jr.
Hubert Humphrey
John Lindsay

Republicans
Dwight Eisenhower
John Foster Dulles
Thomas E. Dewey
Jacob Javits
Paul Hoffman
Robert McNamara
John Gardner
Henry Cabot Lodge
Rockefellers
Elliot Richardson
Arthur Burns
Henry Kissinger
Richard Nixon

The following are so-called Democrats who have been or now are C.F.R. agents: Dean Acheson, Alger Hiss, Adlai Stevenson, John Kennedy, Robert Kennedy, Edward Kennedy,* Averell Harriman, George Ball, Henry Fowler, Dean Rusk, Adam Yarmolinsky, Hubert Humphrey and John Lindsay.

It is interesting to note that rewards of cushy jobs were given by the international bankers to many men high in the LBJ administration for their services. Undersecretary of State George Ball went with Lehman Brothers; Secretary of the Treasury Henry Fowler was taken in by Goldman, Sachs & Co.; Budget Director Peter Lewis, Undersecretary of the Treasury Frederick Deming and former Secretary of Commerce C. R. Smith all avoided the bread lines by being picked up by Lazard Freres (Rothschilds). Fowler and Deming were largely responsible for policies which led to European nations claiming half of our gold (and having potential claims on the rest) as well as denuding the U. S. Treasury of all of the silver reserves it had built up over a century of time. Did the international bankers take pity on these men for their incompetence or were they rewarded for a job well done?

Controlling the Republican Party for the C.F.R. have been Dwight D. Eisenhower, John Foster Dulles, Thomas E. Dewey, Jacob Javits, Robert McNamara, Henry Cabot Lodge, Paul Hoffman, John Gardner, the Rockefeller clan, Elliot Richardson, Arthur Burns, Henry Kissinger and Richard Nixon.**

While it is true that every administration since FDR has been dominated by the C.F.R., the Nixon Adminis-

---

(*Boston Committee)
(**Richard Nixon now claims that he no longer belongs to the C.F.R., having dropped out when the organization became an issue in his primary campaign for the governorship of California in 1962. Nixon has never said why he dropped out, but the fact that he has appointed over 110 C.F.R. members to important positions in his administration speaks for itself. It should come as no surprise that the very same Richard Nixon who campaigned in 1968 as a conservative had already made his real position very clear to the *Insiders* of the C.F.R. by authoring an article in the C.F.R. magazine, *Foreign Affairs,* in October 1967. The title of

tration has set the all-time record by appointing over 110 C.F.R. members to key positions. Henry Kissinger, the "Colonel" House of the Nixon Administration, came to his job directly from employment on the C.F.R. staff. Kissinger represents the very opposite of everything Nixon said he stood for in his campaign. Both Liberals and Conservatives admit Kissinger is by far the most important man in the Nixon Administration.

Adminstrations, both Democrat and Republican, come and go—but the C.F.R. lingers on. This is why the more things seem to change, the more they remain the same. The fix is in at the top, where the same coterie of *Insiders,* bent on control of the world, runs the show. As Professor Quigley admits:

> "There does exist, and has existed for a generation, an international . . . network which operates, to some extent, in the way the radical Right believes the Communists act. In fact, this network, which we may identify as the Round Table Groups, *has no aversion to cooperating with the Communists, or any other groups, and frequently does so."* [Emphasis added.]

Yes, the *Insiders* have no aversion to working with the Communists whose ostensible goal is to destroy them. While the *Insiders* are serving champagne and caviar to their guests in their summer mansions at Newport, or entertaining other members of the social elite aboard their yachts, their agents are out enslaving and murdering people. And you are next on their list.

Clearly, the *Chicago Tribune's* editorial of December 9, 1950, on the C.F.R. still applies:

> "The members of the council [On Foreign Rela-

---

this article, "Asia after Vietnam," revealed how the aspiring President Nixon would open a new policy toward Red China and bring "realism" to our Asian foreign policy.

The C.F.R.'s Annual Report for 1952, admitted that sometimes members in sensitive positions were forced to go underground and keep the membership secret.)

tions] are persons of much more than average influence in their community. They have used the prestige that their wealth, their social position, and their education have given them to lead their country toward bankrupty and military debacle. They should look at their hands. There is blood on them—the dried blood of the last war and the fresh blood of the present one [the Korean War]."

It goes without saying that the C.F.R.'s hands are bloodier now with the gore of 50,000 Americans in Vietnam. Shamefully the Council has succeeded in promoting, as American policy, the shipment of American aid and trade to the East European arsenal of the Viet Cong for the killing of our sons in the field.

It should not be surprising to learn that there is on the international level an organizational equivalent of the C.F.R. This group calls itself the Bilderbergers. If scarcely one American in a thousand has any familiarity with the C.F.R., it is doubtful that one in five thousand has any knowledge of the Bilderbergers. Again, this is not accidental.

The strange name of this group is taken from the site of the first meeting in May, 1954—the Hotel de Bilderberg—in Oostebeek, Holland. The man who created the Bilderbergers is His Royal Highness Prince Bernhard of the Netherlands. The Prince is an important figure in Royal Dutch Petroleum (Shell Oil) and the Societe General de Belgique, a huge conglomerate cartel with worldwide holdings. The Bilderbergers meet once—or sometimes twice—a year. Those in attendance include leading political and financial figures from the United States and Western Europe. Prince Bernhard makes no effort to hide the fact that the ultimate goal of the Bilderbergers is a world government. In the meantime, while the "new world order" is being built, the Bilderbergers coordinate the efforts of the European and American power elites.

Prince Bernhard's counterpart among the American Bilderbergers is David Rockefeller, chairman of the board of the C.F.R., whose economic base is the giant Chase Manhattan Bank and Standard Oil. Among the other Bilderbergers from the world of ultra-high finance are Baron Edmund de Rothschild of the House of Rothschild, C. Douglas Dillon (C.F.R.) of Dillon Read & Co., Robert McNamara of the World Bank, Sir Eric Roll of S. G. Warburg & Co., Ltd., Pierce Paul Schweitzer of the International Monetary Fund, and George Ball (C.F.R.) of Lehman Brothers.

Not everyone who attends one of the Bilderbergers' secret meetings is an *Insider,* but only men of the Left are allowed to attend the private meetings following the general sessions. The avowedly Socialist Parties of Europe are well represented . . . another example of the tie-in between the *Insiders* of high finance and the ostensible leaders of the proletariat. Bilderberg policy is not planned by those who attend the conferences, but by the elite steering committee of *Insiders* composed of 24 Europeans and 15 Americans. Past and present Americans of the Bilderberger Steering Committee include George W. Ball, Gardner Cowles, John H. Ferguson, Henry J. Heinz II, Robert D. Murphy, David Rockefeller, Shepard Stone, James D. Zellerbach, Emelio G. Collado, Arthur H. Dean, Gabriel Hauge, C. D. Jackson, George Nebolsine, Dean Rusk and General Walter Bedell Smith. Those who adhere to the accidental theory of history will claim that it is sheer coincidence that every single one of those named as past and present members of the Bilderberger Steering Committee is or was a member of the Council on Foreign Relations.

The Bilderberger Advisory Committee forms an even more "inner circle" than the Steering Committee. Americans on the Advisory Committee include Joseph E. Johnson, Dean Rusk, Arthur H. Dean, George Nebolsine, John S. Coleman, General Walter Bedell Smith and Henry J. Heinz II. Again, all are members of the C.F.R.

One would assume (that is, if one had not read this book) that when the world's leading parliamentarians and international tycoons meet to discuss the planning of their

Prince Bernhard of the Netherlands, head of the secret, one world Bilderberger movement, confers with President Nixon. A former Nazi SS storm trooper ("We had a lot of fun"), Bernhard now works with the Rothschilds and Communists to promote a World Super State of the elite. Bernhard holds yearly secret meetings with high U. S. officials, bankers and industrialists to map plans for merging the U. S. and the Soviet Union into a world government. After last meeting, Nixon devalued the dollar and opened up trade with Red China.

Edmond and Guy de Rothschild, leaders of the French Rothschild clan. The Rothschilds are closely connected with Prince Bernhard in business (Royal Dutch Shell) and in the building of a one world super-government with the Soviets. **Time** of Dec. 20, 1963, says of Guy: "Guy is every inch a Rothschild. He personifies much of what the family name stands for . . . He is a friend and confidante of some of France's politicians. . . . Most of all, he is dedicated to enlarging the fortune of his bank. . . . Guy heads a versatile clan of modern day Rothschilds." Edmond, reputedly the richest of the French Rothschilds, is worth $500 million personally, according to estimates.

various nations' foreign policies, that the newshawks from papers and televisionland would be screaming to high heaven that such an event held in secret makes a mockery of the democratic process. One might expect Walter Cronkite to be thundering in wrath about an elite clique meeting to plan our lives; or the *New York Times* editorialists to be pounding their smoking typewriters, fuming about "the public's right to know." But, of course, the landscape painters merely brush the Bilderbergers right out of existence and focus the public's attention on something like the conditions in the prisons or coke bottles littering the highways. Since the Bilderbergers are a group of the Left (or, as the Liberals in the media might say, but don't, "a group of progressives") they are allowed to go on in peace and quiet planning for 1984. The fact that there is heavy Rockefeller (Chase Manhattan Bank and C.F.R.) influence in the media might also have something to do with the fact that while everybody has heard of, say, The John Birch Society (and almost always in a derogatory manner from the Eastern Establishment media), practically nobody has heard of the Bilderbergers.

As this is written, there have been 29 Bilderberger meetings to date. They usually last three days and are held in remote, but plush quarters. The participants are housed in one location and are protected by a thorough security network. Decisions are reached, resolutions adopted, plans of action initiated, but only Bilderbergers ever know for sure what occurred. We must assume that these people did not congregate merely to discuss their golf scores. The press, naturally, is not allowed to be present, although occasionally a brief press conference is held at the end of the meeting at which time the news media are given in very general terms the Bilderberger version of what was discussed. Why all the secrecy if there is really nothing to hide? Why do the Ford, Rockefeller and Carnegie foundations finance the meetings if they are not important? Yes, why?

The most recent meeting took place at Laurance Rockefeller's Woodstock Inn at Woodstock, Vermont, April 23,

24, 25, 1971. Apparently the only newspaper to carry a substantial story on the meeting was the Rutland, Vermont, *Herald,* whose reporter could acquire only sketchy information about what the meeting was all about. The April 20, 1971 issue of the *Herald* reported:

"A rather tight lid of secrecy was being kept on the conference. . . . A closed-door meeting was held in Woodstock last week to brief a handful of local officials on some phases of the conference. One participant of the meeting insisted Monday that the officials were told the meeting would be an 'international peace conference.' However, other reliable sources said the conference will deal with international finance. . . .

The Woodstock Inn will apparently be sealed up like Fort Knox. . . . No press coverage will be allowed, with the exception of issuing a statement at the close of the meeting on Sunday."

When Prince Bernhard arrived at Boston's Logan Airport, he did admit to reporters that the subject of the conference would be the "change in the world-role of the United States." Isn't it nice to have changes in America's role in the world decided upon by Bernhard, Rothschild and Rockefeller? There is real democracy in action, as they say. Present at the scene to carry back orders to Mr. Nixon was C.F.R.-Rockefeller errand boy, the President's Number One advisor on foreign affairs, Henry Kissinger. Shortly after the Woodstock meeting, two ominous and "role changing" events occurred: Henry Kissinger went to Peking and arranged for the acceptance of Red China as a member of the family of trading nations; and an international monetary crisis developed after which the dollar was devalued. As the British statesman and Rothschild confidante Benjamin Disraeli wrote in *Coningsby:* "So you see, my dear Coningsby, that the world is governed by very different personages from what is imagined by those who are not behind the scenes."

CHAPTER SIX

THE ROCKEFELLERS AND THE REDS

The most important Americans of those "different personages" who run the world from behind the scenes are the Rockefellers. The Rockefeller clan reportedly has worked with the Rothschilds and their agents since the 1880's when the original John D. arranged to get a rebate on every barrel of oil he and his competitors shipped over Kuhn, Loeb & Co.-controlled Pennsylvania and Baltimore & Ohio railroads. It has been a profitable partnership ever since, although there appear to have been areas in which the two financial dynasties competed.

The involvement of the Rockefellers with their supposed blood enemies, the Communists, dates back to the Bolshevik Revolution. During the 1920's Lenin established his New Economic Policy (the same name Mr. Nixon applied to his wage-price control package), when the supposedly hated capitalists were invited back into Russia.

The Federal Reserve-CFR *Insiders* began pushing to open up Communist Russia to U. S. traders soon after the revolution. However, at that time public opinion ran so high against the Bolsheviks because of their barbarism that it was official U. S. government policy not to deal with the outlaw government. The U. S. did not officially recognize the Bolsheviks until 1933. In the meantime, the Soviet economy was in a shambles and the people were starving to death. Communism would have collapsed had it not been aided by the *Insiders*. The Bolsheviks were originally saved from collapse by Herbert Hoover (CFR) who raised money to buy food which was appropriated by Lenin and his gangsters. They used it as a tool to subdue starving peasants who had been resisting their newly imposed slave masters. While Hoover's "humanitarian" gesture saved the Soviet regime, the Russian economy was still in total chaos. In came the Vanderlips,

Harrimans and Rockefellers. One of the first to jump in was Frank Vanderlip, an agent of the Rockefellers and one of the Jekyl Island conspirators, president of the Rockefeller First National City Bank, who compared Lenin to George Washington. (Louis Budenz, *The Bolshevik Invasion Of The West,* Bookmailer, p. 115)

The Rockefellers assigned their public relations agent, Ivy Lee, to sell the American public the idea that the Bolsheviks were merely misunderstood idealists who were actually kind benefactors of mankind.

Professor Antony Sutton of Stanford University's Hoover Institution, notes in his highly authorative *Western Technology and Soviet Economic Development:*

"Quite predictably, 180 pages later, Lee concludes that the communist problem is merely psychological. By this time he is talking about 'Russians' (not Communists) and concludes 'they are all right.' He suggests the United States should not engage in propaganda; makes a plea for peaceful coexistence; and suggests the United States would find it sound policy to recognize the USSR and advance credits." (Antony Sutton, *Western Technology and Soviet Economic Development, 1917-1930,* Hoover Institution on War, Revolution and Peace, Stanford University, Calif., 1968, p. 292)

After the Bolshevik Revolution, Standard of New Jersey bought 50 per cent of the Nobel's huge Caucasus oil fields even though the property had theoretically been nationalized. (O'Connor, Harvey, *The Empire Of Oil,* Monthly Review Press, New York, 1955, p. 270.)

In 1927, Standard Oil of New York built a refinery in Russia, thereby helping the Bolsheviks put their economy back on its feet. Professor Sutton states: "This was the first United States investment in Russia since the Revolution." (Ibid, Vol. 1, p. 38)

Shortly thereafter Standard Oil of New York and its subsidiary, Vacuum Oil Company, concluded a deal to market Soviet oil in European countries and it was reported that a loan of $75,000,000 to the Bolsheviks was arranged. *(National Republic,* Sept. 1927.)

We have been unable to find out if Standard Oil was even theoretically expropriated by the Communists. Sutton writes:

> "Only the Danish telegraph concessions, the Japanese fishing, coal and oil concessions, and the Standard Oil lease remained after 1935." (Ibid, Vol. II, p. 17.)

Wherever Standard Oil would go, Chase National Bank was sure to follow. (The Rockefeller's Chase Bank was later merged with the Warburg's Manhattan Bank to form the present Chase Manhattan Bank.) In order to rescue the Bolsheviks, who were supposedly an archenemy, the Chase National Bank was instrumental in establishing the American-Russian Chamber of Commerce in 1922. President of the Chamber was Reeve Schley, a vice-president of Chase National Bank. (Ibid, Vol. II, p. 288) According to Professor Sutton: "In 1925, negotiations between Chase and Prombank extended beyond the finance of raw materials and mapped out a complete program for financing Soviet raw material exports to the U. S. and imports of U. S. cotton and machinery. (Ibid, Vol. II, p. 226) Sutton also reports that "Chase National Bank and the Equitable Trust Company were leaders in the Soviet credit business." (Ibid, p. 277)

The Rockefeller's Chase National Bank also was involved in selling Bolshevik bonds in the United States in 1928. Patriotic organizations denounced the Chase as an "international fence." Chase was called "a disgrace to America. . . . They will go to any lengths for a few dollars profits." (Ibid, Vol. II, p. 291) Congressman Louis McFadden, chairman of the House Banking Committee, maintained in a speech to his fellow Congressmen:

> "The Soviet government has been given United

States Treasury funds by the Federal Reserve Board and the Federal Reserve Banks acting through the Chase Bank and the Guaranty Trust Company and other banks in New York City. . . .

. . . Open up the books of Amtorg, the trading organization of the Soviet government in New York, and of Gostorg, the general office of the Soviet Trade Organization, and of the State Bank of the Union of Soviet Socialist Republics and you will be staggered to see how much American money has been taken from the United States' Treasury for the benefit of Russia. Find out what business has been transacted for the State Bank of Soviet Russia by its correspondent, the Chase Bank of New York; . . . ." *(Congressional Record,* June 15, 1933.)

But the Rockefellers apparently were not alone in financing the Communist arm of the *Insiders'* conspiracy. According to Professor Sutton ". . . there is a report in the State Department files that names Kuhn, Loeb & Co. (the long-established and important financial house in New York) as the financier of the First Five Year Plan. See U. S. State Dept. Decimal File, 811.51/3711 and 861.50 FIVE YEAR PLAN/236." (Sutton, op. cit., Vol. II, p. 340n.)

Professor Sutton proves conclusively in his three volume history of Soviet technological development that the Soviet Union was almost literally manufactured by the U.S.A. Sutton quotes a report by Averell Harriman to the State Department in June, 1944 as stating:

"Stalin paid tribute to the assistance rendered by the United States to Soviet industry before and during the war. He said that about two-thirds of all the large industrial enterprise in the Soviet Union had been built with United States help or technical assistance." (Sutton, op. cit., Vol. II, p. 3.)

Remember that this was at a time when the Soviets had

already established an extensive spy network in the U. S. and the Communist *Daily Worker* newspaper regularly called for the destruction of our liberty and the Sovietizing of America.

Sutton shows that there is hardly a segment of the Soviet economy which is not a result of the transference of Western, particularly American, technology.

This cannot be wholly the result of accident. For fifty years the Federal Reserve-CFR-Rockefeller-*Insider* crowd has advocated and carried out policies aimed at increasing the power of their satellite, the Soviet Union. Meanwhile, America spends $75 billion a year on defense to protect itself from the enemy the *Insiders* are building up.

What has been true of the past is even more valid today. The leader in promoting the transfer of technology and increasing aid and trade with the Communists is the Council on Foreign Relations.

On October 7, 1966, President Lyndon Johnson, a man who had appointed a C.F.R. member to virtually every strategic position in his administration, stated:

"We intend to press for legislative authority to negotiate trade agreements which could extend most-favored-nation tariff treatment to European Communist states. . . .

We will reduce export controls on East-West trade with respect to hundreds of non-strategic items. . . ."
The *New York Times* reported one week later on —October 13, 1966:

"The United States put into effect today one of President Johnson's proposals for stimulating East-West trade by removing restrictions on the export of more than four hundred commodities to the Soviet Union and Eastern Europe. . . .

Among the categories from which items have been selected for export relaxation are vegetables, cereals, fodder, hides, crude and manufactured rubber, pulp and waste paper, textiles and textile fibers, crude fertilizers, metal ores and scrap, petroleum, gas and derivatives, chemical compounds and products, dyes, medicines, fireworks, detergents, plastic materials, metal products and machinery, and scientific and professional instruments."

Virtually every one of these "non-strategic" items has a direct or indirect use in war. Later, items such as rifle cleaning compounds, electronic equipment and radar were declared "non-strategic" and cleared for shipment to the Soviet Union. The trick simply is to declare almost everything "non-strategic." A machine gun is still considered strategic and therefore may not be shipped to the Communists, but the tools for making the machine guns and the chemicals to propel the bullets have been declared "non-strategic." Meanwhile, nearly 50,000 Americans have died in Vietnam. The Viet Cong and North Vietnamese receive 85 percent of their war materials from Russia and the Soviet bloc nations. Since their economies are incapable of supporting a war, the Communist arm of the conspiracy needed help from the Finance Capitalist arm. The United States has been financing and equipping both sides of the terrible Vietnamese war, killing our own soldiers by proxy. Again, the landscape painters in the mass media have kept the American public from learning this provable fact.

Not surprisingly, the Rockefellers have been leaders in championing this bloody trade. On January 16, 1967, one of the most incredible articles ever to appear in a newspaper graced the front page of the Establishment's daily, the *New York Times*. Under the headline "Eaton Joins Rockefellers To Spur Trade With Reds" the article stated:

> "An alliance of family fortunes linking Wall Street and the Midwest is going to try to build economic bridges between the free world and Communist Europe.
> The International Basic Economy Corporation, controlled by the Rockefeller brothers, and Tower International, Inc., headed by Cyrus S. Eaton Jr.,

Cleveland financier, plan to cooperate in promoting trade between the Iron Curtain countries, including the Soviet Union. . . ."

International Basic Economy Corporation (IBEC) is run by Richard Aldrich, grandson of Federal Reserve plotter Nelson Aldrich, and Rodman Rockefeller (CFR), Rocky's son. On October 20, 1969, IBEC announced that N. M. Rothschild & Sons of London had entered into partnership with the firm.

Cyrus Eaton Jr. is the son of the notoriously pro-Soviet Cyrus Eaton, who began his career as secretary to John D. Rockefeller. It is believed that Eaton's rise to power in finance resulted from backing by his mentor. The agreement between Tower International and IBEC continues an old alliance. Although Eaton's name does not appear on the CFR's membership rolls, the Reece Committee which investigated foundations for Congress in 1953, found that Eaton was a secret member.

Among the "non-strategic" items which the Rockefeller-Eaton axis is going to build for the Communists are ten rubber goods plants, including two synthetic rubber plants worth $200 million. Mr. Eaton explains in the *Times* article: "These people are setting up new automobile plants and know they have got to have tire factories." Under the Nixon Administration which, contrary to campaign promises, has multiplied trade with the Reds tenfold, American concerns are building the world's largest truck factory for the Communists. Trucks are necessary for a nation's war machine and truck factories can be converted to the production of tanks as was done during WWII. The U. S. will provide the Soviets with both the facilities to build the trucks and the tires (or tank treads) for them to roll on.

In addition, the Rockefellers and Eatons are constructing a $50 million aluminum producing plant for the Reds. Aluminum for jet planes is considered "non-strategic" under Johnson-Nixon doctrine.

Even more incredibly, the *Times* reveals:

Nelson Rockefeller greets Khrushchev, the infamous "Butcher of Budapest." The Rockefeller and Eaton families have now joined forces to build war production plants behind the Iron Curtain so that the Communists can become a bigger threat to U. S. survival. America spends $70 billion a year ostensibly on defense and then the Rockefellers build aluminum mills for the Communists. Only the absence of a formal declaration of war in Vietnam keeps the Eatons and Rockefellers from being actionable for treason. They have the blood of nearly 50,000 American servicemen on their hands.

When Communist dictators visit the U. S. they do not visit laborers or union leaders, but hob-nob with industrial leaders. There is little, if any, attempt by the Red dictators to identify with the working class. Here Nikita Khrushchev greets the avowedly pro-Communist industrialist Cyrus Eaton. Eaton started his business career as secretary to John D. Rockefeller and the Rockefeller family is believed to be largely responsible for his fortune.

"Last month, Tower International reached a tentative agreement with the Soviet patent and licensing organization, Licensintorg, covering future licensing and patent transactions. Until now, Mr. Eaton said, the Russians have left the buying and selling of licenses and patents to the Amtorg Trading Corporation, the official Soviet agency in this country for promoting Soviet-American trade."

This means that the Rockefellers and Eatons have a monopoly on the transfer of technological capability to the supposed enemies of the super-rich, the Soviet Union. According to the *Times:*

"Mr. Eaton acknowledged the difficulties that Amtorg's representatives had encountered here in trying to arrange licensing agreements with American companies. 'As you can imagine,' he said, 'it is almost impossible for a Russian to walk into the research department of an American aerospace company and try to arrange the purchase of a patent'."

Certainly every loyal American will say to himself, "Well, I would hope to God the Soviets couldn't walk into our defense plants and buy a patent." The Rockefellers and the Eatons have solved that problem for the Communists. Now, instead of dealing with an official agency of the Soviet government, American concerns will be dealing with the Rockefellers. Meanwhile, nearly 50,000 Americans have died in Vietnam, many of them killed by weapons which the Rockefellers directly or indirectly supplied to our avowed enemies. Only the technicality of the lack of a formal declaration of war prevents the Rockefellers' trading in the blood of dead Americans from being actionable as treason.

Thus by the purchase of patents for the Communists the Rockefellers are virtually in charge of research and development for the Soviet military machine, allowing the Soviets to mass produce American developments. The transfer of such knowledge is even more important than the sale of weapons. A process that may have taken an American corporation a decade to develop is transferred *in toto* to the Communists. Does it make sense to spend $75 billion a year on national defense and then deliberately increase the war-making potential of an avowed enemy? It does to Mr. Rockefeller and the *Insiders*.

Since the Rockefellers have contracted to arrange for patents for the Soviets, they are by dictionary definition Communist agents. Would it not be more accurate to define the Communists as Rockefeller agents?

Indicative of this was a strange event which occurred in October of 1964. David Rockefeller, president of the Chase Manhattan Bank and chairman of the board of the Council on Foreign Relations, took a vacation in the Soviet Union. This is a peculiar place for the world's greatest "imperialist" to take his vacation since much of Communist propaganda deals with taking all of David's wealth away from him and distributing it to "the people." A few days after Rockefeller ended his "vacation" in the Kremlin, Nikita Khrushchev was recalled from a vacation at a Black Sea resort to learn that he had been fired. How strange! As far as the world knew, Khrushchev was the absolute dictator of the Soviet government and, more important, head of the Communist Party which runs the USSR. Who has the power to fire the man who was supposedly the absolute dictator? Did David Rockefeller journey to the Soviet Union to fire an employee? Obviously the position of premier in the Soviet Union is a figurehead with the true power residing elsewhere. Perhaps in New York.

For five decades the Communists have based their propaganda on the theme that they were going to destroy the Rockefellers and the other super-rich. Yet we find that for five decades the Rockefellers have been involved in building the strength of the Soviets. We are supposed to believe those international cartelists do this because they are foolish or greedy. Does this make sense? If a criminal goes up and down the streets shouting at the top of his lungs that as soon as he gets hold of a gun he is going to kill Joe Doaks, and you learn that Doaks is secretly giving guns to the criminal, one of two things must be true. Either Doaks is a fool or all the shouting is just "show biz" and the criminal secretly works for Doaks. The Rockefellers are not fools.

While David runs the financial end of the Rockefeller dynasty, Nelson runs the political. Nelson would like to be President of the United States. But, unfortunately for him, he is unacceptable to the vast majority of the grass roots of his own party. The next best thing to being President is controlling a President. Nelson Rockefeller and Richard Nixon are supposed to be bitter political competitors. In a sense they are, but that still does not preclude Rockefeller from asserting dominion over Mr. Nixon. When Mr. Nixon and Mr. Rockefeller competed for the Republican nomination in 1968, Rockefeller naturally would have preferred to win the prize, but regardless of who won, he would control the highest office in the land.

You will recall that right in the middle of drawing up the Republican platform in 1960, Mr. Nixon suddenly left Chicago and flew to New York to meet with Nelson Rockefeller in what Barry Goldwater described as the "Munich of the Republican Party." There was no political reason why Mr. Nixon needed to crawl to Mr. Rockefeller. He had the convention all sewed up. The *Chicago Tribune* cracked that it was like Grant surrendering to Lee.

In *The Making of the President, 1960,* Theodore White noted that Nixon accepted all the Rockefeller terms for this meeting, including provisions "that Nixon telephone Rockefeller personally with his request for a meeting; that they meet at the Rockefeller apartment. . . that their meeting be secret and later be announced in a press release from the Governor, not Nixon; that the meeting be clearly announced as taking place at the Vice President's request; that the statement of policy issuing from it be long, detailed, inclusive, not a summary communiqué."

The meeting produced the infamous "Compact of Fifth Avenue" in which the Republican Platform was scrapped and replaced by Rockefeller's socialist plans. The *Wall Street Journal* of July 25, 1960, commented: ". . . a little band of conservatives within the party . . . are shoved to the sidelines. . . . [T]he fourteen points are very liberal indeed; they comprise a platform akin in many ways to the Democratic platform and they are a far cry from the things that conservative men think the Republican Party ought to stand for. . . ." As Theodore White put it:

> "Never had the quadrennial liberal swoop of the regulars been more nakedly dramatized than by the open compact of Fifth Avenue. Whatever honor they might have been able to carry from their services on the platform committee had been wiped out. A single night's meeting of the two men in a millionaire's triplex apartment in Babylon-by-the-Hudson, eight hundred and thirty miles away, was about to overrule them; they were exposed as clowns for all the world to see."

The whole story behind what happened in Rockefeller's apartment will doubtless never be known. We can only make an educated guess in light of subsequent events. But it is obvious that since that time Mr. Nixon has been in the Rockefeller orbit.

After losing to Kennedy by an eyelash, Mr. Nixon, against his wishes, and at the request (or order) of Rockefeller, entered the California gubernatorial race and lost. (For further details see the author's *Richard Nixon: The Man Behind The Mask.*) After losing to Pat Brown in the California gubernatorial race in 1962, Nixon had universally been consigned to the political trash heap. He left his practice as an attorney in California and went to New York, where he moved in as a neighbor of Nelson Rockefeller, the man who is supposedly his archenemy, in a $100,000-a-year apartment in a building owned by Rockefeller. Then Mr. Nixon went to work for the law firm of Mr. Rockefeller's personal attorney, John Mitchell, and in the next six years spent most of his time touring the country and the world, first rebuilding his political reputation and then campaigning to get the 1968 Republican nomination. At the same time, according to his own financial statement, his net worth multiplied many times and he became quite wealthy. Nelson Rockefeller, (and his colleagues of the Eastern Liberal Establishment), who helped make Nixon acceptable to Conservatives by appearing to oppose him, rescued Nixon from political oblivion and made him President of the United States. Does it not make sense that Mr. Nixon, the man of passionate ambition whose career had sunk to the bottom, had to make some deals in order to reach his goal? And did he not acquire massive political debts in return for being made President by the Eastern Liberal Establishment?

When Nixon left Washington, he, by his own claim, had little more than an old Oldsmobile automobile, Pat's respectable Republican cloth coat, and a government pension. While in law practice Nixon had an income of $200,-000 per year, of which more than half went to pay for the apartment in Rocky's building. By 1968, he reported his net worth as $515,830, while assigning a value of only $45,000 to his partnership in his increasingly flourishing law firm. It may be that the frugal Mr. Nixon acquired the after-tax investment capital that mushroomed into $858,190 in assets by faithfully plugging his change into a piggy bank. Then again, it may have been part of Nixon's deal with Rockefeller and the *Insiders* that Mr. Nixon's personal poverty problems should be solved. The President is obviously an un-free agent.

The man most observers agree is the most powerful man in the Administration on domestic policy matters is Attorney General John Mitchell. Mitchell, who had been a Nixon law partner, served as campaign manager in 1968, and reportedly will serve in that capacity in 1972. The *Wall Street Journal* of January 17, 1969, revealed that Mitchell was Rocky's personal lawyer. The Establishment's landscape painters have etched a picture of Mitchell as a tough cop-type conservative bent; it appears that in reality Mitchell is but another Rockefeller agent.

Richard Nixon was elected President on a platform which promised to stop America's retreat before world Communism. Yet he appointed Henry Kissinger, a man who represented the opposite of the stands Mr. Nixon took during his campaign, to a position which is virtually Assistant President. Is it surprising then that Mr. Nixon has done just the opposite of what he promised he would do during his 1968 campaign?

How did Mr. Nixon come to pick an ultra-liberal to be his number one foreign policy advisor? We are told by *Time* magazine that Mr. Nixon met Kissinger at a cocktail party given by Clare Boothe Luce during the Christmas holidays in 1967. Mr. Nixon is supposed to have been so impressed by Dr. Kissinger's cocktail party repartee that he appointed him to the most powerful position in the Nixon Administration. Mr. Nixon would have to be stupid to have done that; and Mr. Nixon is not stupid. The Kissinger appointment was arranged by Nelson Rockefeller. (Salt Lake City *Deseret News,* March 27, 1970.) Kissinger had served for five years as Rockefeller's personal advisor on foreign affairs and at the time of his appointment he was serving as a paid staff member of the Council on Foreign Relations.

Mr. Nixon's fantastic about face was praised by LBJ in the *Washington Star* of Dec. 1, 1971. The paper states:

"Former President Lyndon B. Johnson acknowledges that Richard Nixon, as a Republican President, has been able to accomplish some things that a Democratic President could not have. . . .

" 'Can't you just see the uproar,' he asked during a recent interview, 'if I had been responsible for Taiwan getting kicked out of the United Nations? Or if I had imposed sweeping national controls on prices and wages?'

" 'Nixon has gotten by with it,' he observed, an appreciative tone in his voice. 'If I had tried to do it, or Truman, or Humphrey, or any Democrat, we would have been clobbered.' "

Nelson Rockefeller and Richard Nixon are theoretically political enemies, but Rocky arranged '68 election so that if he could not be President, someone whom he controlled would be. The Rockefeller family, through their Chase Manhattan Bank and other entities, have been great benefactors of the Soviet Union ever since Communist Revolution in Russia. During campaign Nixon promised to halt shipment of war materials from America to North Vietnam via European Communist bloc because these supplies were being used to kill American soldiers. But much of this bloc trade is controlled by Rockefellers and Nixon has reversed himself and greatly multiplied such trade. The press, quite naturally, remains silent about killing American soldiers by proxy.

The boss and his two employees—the three musketeers of the CFR—Rocky, President Nixon and Henry Kissinger confer. Kissinger of Harvard was made virtual Assistant President by Rockefeller on whose staff he had served for a dozen years. Kissinger also had been on the staff of the CFR just prior to joining the Nixon Administration. Kissinger was the very embodiment of everything Nixon denounced during his '68 campaign. This explains why Nixon has reversed himself on so many stands. Among those to hail Mr. Nixon's move to the Left is Alger Hiss, the Communist spy Richard Nixon helped convict. (**Chicago Tribune**, Oct. 25, 1971.) It was the Hiss Case which catapulted Nixon from obscurity into the Senate, the Vice Presidency and, eventually, the White House.

CHAPTER SEVEN

PRESSURE FROM ABOVE AND PRESSURE FROM BELOW

The Establishment's official landscape artists have done a marvelous job of painting a picture of Richard Nixon as a conservative. Unfortunately, this picture is twenty years out of date. The very liberal Senator Hugh Scott of Pennsylvania boasted to a reporter one day: "[Liberals] get the action and the Conservatives get the rhetoric." Richard Nixon could not have been elected had he run as a Rockefeller liberal, but he can get away with running his Administration like one simply because the landscape painters fail to call the public's attention to the fact. However, columnist Stewart Alsop in writing for a sophisticated audience of approving Liberals, reveals the real Nixon. Alsop claims that if Nixon were judged by his deeds instead of his ancient image, the Liberals' attitude toward him would be different. If only the Liberals' Pavlovian response to the Nixon name could be eliminated, says Alsop, they would realize how far Left he is. Therefore Alsop substitutes a hypothetical "President Liberal" for President Nixon:

> ". . . If President Liberal were actually in the White House, it is not at all hard to imagine the reaction to his program. The right would be assailing President Liberal for bugging out of Vietnam, undermining American defenses, fiscal irresponsibility, and galloping socialism. The four basic Presidential policy positions listed above would be greeted with hosannas by the liberals. . . .
>
> Instead, the liberals have showered the President with dead cats, while most conservatives have maintained a glum silence, and thus the Administration has been 'little credited' for 'much genuine achieve-

ment.' But there are certain special reasons, which Pat Moynihan omitted to mention, why this is so."

Alsop further explains how having the reputation of being an enemy of the Liberal Democrats helps Nixon pass their program:

"For one thing, there is a sort of unconscious conspiracy between the President and his natural enemies, the liberal Democrats, to conceal the extent to which his basic program, leaving aside frills and rhetoric, is really the liberal Democratic program. Richard Nixon is the first professional politician and 'real Republican' to be elected President in 40 years—and it is not in the self-interest of the liberals to give credit to such a President for liberal initiatives. By the same token, it is not in the self-interest of the President to risk his conservative constituency by encouraging the notion that he is not a 'real Republican' after all, but a liberal Democrat at cut rates. . . .

There are plenty of examples of the mutual obfuscation which results from this mutual interest. The withdrawal of half a million men from Vietnam is quite obviously the greatest retreat in American history. But the President talks as though it were somehow a glorious advance, certain to guarantee a 'just and lasting peace.' When the President—like any commander of a retreat—resorts to spoiling actions to protect his dwindling rear guard, the liberals howl that he is 'chasing the will-o'-the-wisp of military victory.'

. . . When the President cuts back real military strength more sharply than in a quarter of a century, the liberals attack him for failing to 'reorder priorities.' The President, in his rhetoric about a 'strong defense,' plays the same game. The result, as John Kenneth Galbraith accurately noted recently, is that 'most people and maybe most congressmen think the Administration is indulging the Pentagon even more than the Democrats,' which is the precise opposite of the truth. . . ."

Alsop continued what is probably the most damning column ever written about Richard Nixon by noting the role that the mass media have played in portraying to the public an image that is the reverse of the truth:

". . . There is also a human element in this exercise in mutual obfuscation. To the liberals, especially the liberal commentators who dominate the media, Richard Nixon is Dr. Fell ('The reason why I cannot tell, but this I know and know full well, I do not like thee, Dr. Fell.'). This is not surprising. Not too many years ago, Richard M. Nixon was one of the most effective—and least lovable—of the conservative Republican professionals of the McCarthy era."

The columnist, himself a member of the socialist Americans for Democratic Action (ADA), speculated on what the "old Nixon" would have had to say about the "new Nixon":

". . . on his past record, it is not at all hard to imagine R. M. Nixon leading the assault on the President for his 'bug-out,' 'fiscal irresponsibility,' 'galloping socialism,' and all the rest of it. So how can one expect Mr. Nixon to defend President Liberal's program with the passionate conviction that a President Robert Kennedy, say, would have brought to the defense of such a program?"

Alsop has revealed the *real* Nixon and is obviously pleased. Those who voted for Nixon shouldn't be quite so happy. If you liked the Richard Nixon who ran for the Presidency, then you cannot, if you are consistent, like the Richard Nixon who is President. Nixon and his fellow "moderates" have turned the Republican elephant into a donkey in elephant's clothing. On June 19, 1959, Vice President Nixon gloated: "In summary, the Republican administration produced the things that the Democrats promised." It looks as if it's happening again!

A year and a half earlier Nixon had been warbling a different tune:

> "If we have nothing to offer other than a pale carbon copy of the New Deal, if our only purpose is to gain and retain power, the Republican Party no longer has any reason to exist, and it ought to go out of business."

The Nixon "Game Plan," as Harvard Professor John Kenneth Galbraith gleefully points out, is SOCIALISM. The Nixon "Game Plan" is infinitely more clever and dangerous than those of his predecessors because it masquerades as being the opposite of what it is.

Mr. Nixon is aware that most Americans fear "big government." An August 1968, Gallup Poll showed that 46 per cent of the American public believed that "big government" was the "biggest threat to the country." Gallup commented: "Although big government has been a favorite Republican target for many years, rank and file Democrats are nearly as critical of growing Federal power as are Republicans." Recognizing this attitude, Mr. Nixon geared much of his campaign rhetoric to attacking Big Daddy government. However, the Nixon Administration has taken massive steps to further concentrate authority in the federal "power pinnacle." (See Chart 3, p. 34)

While centralizing power at a rate which would have made Hubert Humphrey blush, Mr. Nixon has continued to pay lip service to decentralization. During the first year of his Administration Mr. Nixon announced his "New Federalism" (the name taken from the title of a book by Nelson Rockefeller). The first part of the "New Federalism" is the Family Assistance Program (FAP) which would, contrary to his campaign promises, provide a Guaranteed Annual Income. Based on suggestions from John Gardner of the C.F.R. and Daniel Moynihan, a member of the board of directors of the socialist ADA, the FAP would double the number on welfare and increase tremendously the power of the executive branch of the federal government. The Leftwing weekly, the *New Republic,* cheered the proposal as "creeping socialism."

The second major segment of the President's "New Federalism" is revenue sharing with the states, touted as a step in the decentralization of power from the federal government. Actually, the program does just the opposite. The money must first go from the states to Washington before it can be shared. As columnist James J. Kilpatrick remarked: ". . . power to control follows the Federal dollar as surely as that famous lamb accompanied little Mary." As soon as the states and local governments get hooked on the federal funds, the controls will be put on just as they were in education and agriculture. Every field the government attempts to take over it first subsidizes. You can't decentralize government by centralizing the tax collections.

Mr. Nixon's "power to the people" slogan really means "power to the President."

House Ways and Means Chairman Wilbur Mills has called the revenue-sharing plan a "trap" that "could become a massive weapon against the independence of state and local government." The plan, said Mills, "goes in the direction of centralized government."

But, Mr. Nixon is very clever. In his 1971 State of the Union Message, the talk in which he used the Communist slogan "Power to the People," the President said:

"We in Washington will at last be able to provide government that is truly for the people. I realize that what I am asking is that not only the Executive branch in Washington, but that even this Congress will have to change by giving up some of its power."

That sounds reasonable doesn't it? The Executive branch will give up some power and the Congress will give up some power and the people will gain by having these powers returned to them. Right? Wrong! That is nothing but verbal sleight of hand. Notice the precision of Mr. Nixon's language. He speaks of the "Executive branch *in Washington*" giving up some of its power. Three days later it became obvious why Mr. Nixon added the seemingly redundant "in Washington" when it was announced that the country was being carved up into ten federal districts. These federal districts would soon be used to administer the wage and price controls which centralize in the federal government almost total power over the economy.

To many political observers the most shocking development of the past year was the admission by President Richard Nixon to newsman Howard K. Smith that he is "now a Keynesian in economics." The jolted Smith commented later, "That's a little like a Christian Crusader saying: 'All things considered, I think Mohammed was right.' " Howard K. Smith was well aware that such a statement was tantamount to a declaration by Mr. Nixon that "I am now a Socialist." John Maynard Keynes, the English economist and Fabian Socialist, bragged that he was promoting the "euthanasia of capitalism."

It is generally believed in England among students of this conspiracy that John Maynard Keynes produced his *General Theory of Money and Credit* at the behest of certain *Insiders* of international finance who hired him to concoct a pseudo-scientific justification for government deficit spending—just as the mysterious League of Just Men had hired Karl Marx to write the *Communist Manifesto*. The farther a government goes into debt, the more interest is paid to the powerful *Insiders* who "create" money to buy government bonds by the simple expedient of bookkeeping entries. Otherwise, you can bet your last farthing that the *Insiders* of international banking would be violently opposed to inflationary deficits.

In his internationally syndicated column of February 3, 1971, James Reston (C.F.R.) exclaimed:

> "The Nixon budget is so complex, so unlike the Nixon of the past, so un-Republican that it defies rational analysis. . . . The Nixon budget is more planned, has more welfare in it, and has a bigger predicted deficit than any other budget of this century."

118

During 1967, while on the primary trail, Richard Nixon made exorbitant Democrat spending his Number Two campaign issue, just behind the failure of the Democrats to win the Vietnam War. Mr. Johnson's 1967 Budget was $158.6 billion, which at the time seemed astronomical. Mr. Nixon claimed that if that amount were not sliced by $10 billion the country faced financial disaster. At a time when the Vietnam War was a far bigger financial drain than it is now, Richard Nixon argued that we should be spending around $150 billion. President Nixon is now spending $230 billion, and bills already introduced in Congress and likely to pass could push the 1972 Fiscal Budget (July 1, 1971 to July 1, 1972) to $250 billion.

The point is that the man who campaigned as Mr. Frugal in 1968 is, in his third year of office, out-spending by $80 to $100 billion what he said his predecessor should spend. And some experts are predicting that Mr. Nixon could spend as much as $275 billion next year.

This is the same Richard Nixon who in Dallas on October 11, 1968, declared that "America cannot afford four years of Hubert Humphrey in the White House" because he had advocated programs which would have caused "a spending spree that would have bankrupted this nation." Candidate Nixon flayed the Johnson Administration for failing "to cut deficit spending which is the cause of our present inflation." Budget deficits, he said, "lie at the heart of our troubles." For his own part, he renounced any "massive step-up" in federal spending. "This is a prescription for further inflation," said Nixon. "I believe it is also a prescription for economic disaster."

While it took LBJ five years to run up a $55 billion deficit, Senator Harry Byrd notes that the accumulated deficit for Mr. Nixon's first *three* years will reach at least $88 billion. Congressional experts are now predicting Richard Nixon could well pour on the red ink to a total of $124 billion in this term of office alone.

In order to halt inflation Mr. Nixon has now instituted wage and price controls. Most Americans, sick of seeing their paychecks shrink in purchasing power each month, have overwhelmingly approved. But this is because most people are not aware of the real causes of inflation. And you can be sure that the Establishment's landscape painters will not explain the truth to them. The truth is that there is a difference beween inflation and the wage-price spiral. When the government runs a deficit, brand new money in the amount of the deficit is put into circulation. As the new money percolates through the economy it bids up wages and prices. This is easy to understand if you think of our economy as a giant auction. Just as at any other auction, if the bidders are suddenly supplied with more money, they will use that money to bid up prices. Inflation, in reality, is an increase in the supply of money. It causes the wage-price spiral which is generally mislabelled *inflation*. You could not have a wage price spiral if you did not have an increase in the money supply with which to pay it. This is not just economics, it is physics. You can't fill a quart bottle with a pint of milk. To say that the wage-price spiral causes inflation is like saying wet streets cause rain. Mr. Nixon, unlike the vast majority of the American public, is aware of the real causes of "inflation." He explained it clearly on January 27, 1970:

> "The inflation we have at the start of the Seventies was caused by heavy deficit spending in the Sixties. In the past decade, the Federal Government spent more than it took in—$57 billion more. These deficits caused prices to rise 25 percent in a decade."

Business blames "inflation" on the unions, and unions blame "inflation" on business, but only the government can cause "inflation."

Mr. Nixon has fastened wage and price controls on the economy supposedly to solve a problem which Mr. Nixon (and LBJ) created by running huge deficits. If he sincerely wanted to stop "inflation" he would have put wage and price controls on the government rather than on the rest of us and would have stopped deficit spending. People are cheering Nixon because he "did something." This

120

is akin to cheering for a motorist who shoots a pedestrian he has just run over.

Wage and price controls are at the very heart of Socialism. You can't have a totalitarian government without wage and price controls and you can't have a free country with them. Why? You cannot impose slavery upon people who have economic freedom. As long as people have economic freedom, they will be free. Wage and price controls are people controls. In his Phase II speech, Mr. Nixon made it clear that the 90-day wage and price controls are with us in one disguise or another from now on. They are a major step towards establishing an all-powerful Executive branch of the federal government.

After the *Insiders* have established the United Socialist States of America (in fact if not in name), the next step is the Great Merger of all nations of the world into a dictatorial world government. This was the main reason behind the push to bring Red China into the United Nations. If you want to control the natural resources, transportation, commerce and banking for the whole world, you must put everybody under the same roof.

The *Insiders'* code word for the world superstate is "new world order," a phrase often used by Richard Nixon. The Council on Foreign Relations states in its *Study No. 7:* "The U. S. must strive to: A. BUILD A NEW INTERNATIONAL ORDER." (Capitals in the original) Establishment spokesman James Reston (CFR) declared in his internationally syndicated column for the *New York Times* of May 21, 1971: "Nixon would obviously like to preside over the creation of a new world order, and believes he has an opportunity to do so in the last 20 months of his first term."

A world government has always been the object of the Communists. In 1915, in No. 40 of the Russian organ, *The Socialist Democrat,* Lenin proposed a "United States of the World." The program of the Communist International of 1936 says that world dictatorship "can be established only by victory of socialism in different coun-

121

tries or groups of countries, after which the Proletariat Republics would unite on federal lines with those already in existence, and this system would expand . . . at length forming the world union of Soviet Socialist Republics."

One of the most important groups promoting the "world union" is the United World Federalists, whose membership is heavily interlocked with that of the Council on Foreign Relations. The UWF advocate turning the UN into a full-fledged world government which would include the Communist nations.

Richard Nixon is, of course, far too clever to actually join the UWF, but he has supported their legislative program since his early days in Congress. In the October 1948 issue of the UWF publication *World Government News,* on page 14, there appears the following announcement: "Richard Nixon: Introduced world government resolution (HCR 68) 1947, and ABC (World Government) resolution 1948."

World government has a strong emotional appeal for Americans, based on their universal desire for world peace. The *Insiders* have the Communists rattling their sabers with one hand and dangling the olive branch with the other. Naturally everyone gravitates towards the olive branch, not realizing that the olive branch is controlled by another arm of the entity that is rattling the sabers.

In September of 1968, candidates for public office received a letter from the United World Federalists that stated:

"Our organization has been endorsed and commended by all U. S. presidents in the last 20 years and by the current nominees for the presidency. As examples we quote as follows:

Richard Nixon: 'Your organization can perform an important service by continuing to emphasize that world peace can only come thru world law. Our goal is world peace. Our instrument for achieving peace will be law and justice. If we concentrate our energies

122

toward these ends, I am hopeful that real progress can be made.'

Hubert Humphrey: 'Every one of us is committed to brotherhood among all nations, but no one pursues these goals with more dignity and dedication than the United World Federalists.' "

There really was not a dime's worth of difference. Voters were given the choice between CFR world government advocate Nixon and CFR world government advocate Humphrey. Only the rhetoric was changed to fool the public.

A world government requires a world supreme court, and Mr. Nixon is on record in favor of a world supreme court. And a world government must have a world police force to enforce the laws of the World Superstate and keep the slaves from rebelling. The *Los Angeles Examiner* of October 28, 1950, reported that Congressman Richard Nixon had introduced a "resolution calling for the establishment of a United Nations police force. . . ."

Not surprisingly, the *Insiders* have their pet planners preparing to administrate their world dictatorship. Under an immense geodetic dome at Southern Illinois University is a completely detailed map of the world which occupies the space of three football fields. Operating under grants from the Ford, Carnegie and Rockefeller foundations (all extensively interlocked with the C.F.R.) a battery of scientists including everything from geographers, psychologists and behavioral scientists to natural scientists, biologists, biochemists and agronomists are making plans to control people. These elite planners conduct exercises in what they call "the world game." For example: There are too many people in Country A and not enough people in Country B. How do you move people from Country A to Country B? We need so many males, so many females, so many of this occupation and so many of that occupation, so many of this age and so many of that age. How do you get these people from Country A and settle them in Country B in the shortest possible time? Another example:

We have an uprising in Country C (or as it would now be called, District C) How long does it take to send in "peace" forces to stop the insurgency?

The World Game people run exercises on global control. If you plan on running the world, you cannot go about it haphazardly. That is why the *Insiders* of the Ford, Carnegie and Rockefeller foundations are making these plans. The real name of the game is *1984*. We will have systematic population reduction, forced sterilization or anything else which the planners deem necessary to establish absolute control in their *humanitarian* utopia. But to enforce these plans, you must have an all-powerful world government. You can't do this if individual nations have sovereignty. And before you can facilitate the Great Merger, you must first centralize control within each nation, destroy the local police and remove the guns from the hands of the citizenry. You must replace our once free Constitutional Republic with an all-powerful central government. And that is exactly what is happening today with the Nixon Administration. Every action of any consequence, despite the smokescreen, has centralized more power in what is rapidly becoming an all-powerful central government.

What we are witnessing is the Communist tactic of *pressure from above and pressure from below,* described by Communist historian Jan Kozak as the device used by the Reds to capture control of Czecho-Slovakia. The pressure from above comes from secret, ostensibly respectable Comrades in the government and Establishment, forming, with the radicalized mobs in the streets below, a giant pincer around middle-class society. The street rioters are pawns, shills, puppets, and dupes for an oligarchy of elitist conspirators working above to turn America's limited government into an unlimited government with total control over our lives and property.

The American middle-class is being squeezed to death by a vise. (See Chart 9) In the streets we have avowed revolutionary groups such as the Students for a Democratic Society (which was started by the League for Industrial Democracy, a group with strong C.F.R. ties), the Black Panthers, the Yippies, the Young Socialist Alliance. These groups chant that if we don't "change" America, we will lose it. "Change" is a word we hear over and over. By "change" these groups mean Socialism. Virtually all members of these groups sincerely believe that they are fighting the Establishment. In reality they are an indispensible ally of the Establishment in fastening Socialism on all of us. The naive radicals think that under Socialism the "people" will run everything. Actually, it will be a clique of *Insiders* in total control, consolidating and controlling all wealth. That is why these schoolboy Lenins and teenage Trotskys are allowed to roam free and are practically never arrested or prosecuted. They are protected. If the Establishment wanted the revolutionaries stopped, how long do you think they would be tolerated?

Chart 9

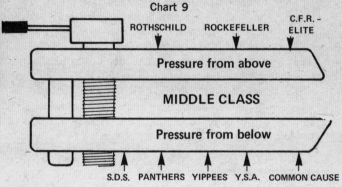

Instead, we find that most of these radicals are the recipients of largesse from major foundations or are receiving money from the government through the War on Poverty. The Rothschild-Rockefeller-C.F.R. *Insiders* at the top "surrender to the demands" for Socialism from the mobs below. The radicals are doing the work of those whom they hate the most.

Remember Bakunin's charge that Marx' followers had one foot in the bank and the other in the Socialist movement.

Further indications of Establishment financing of the Communist S.D.S. are contained in James Kunen's *The Strawberry Statement: Notes of A College Revolutionary.* Describing events at the 1968 S.D.S. national convention, Kunen says:

"Also at the convention, men from Business International Roundtables—the meetings sponsored by Business International for their client groups and heads of government—tried to buy up a few radicals. These men are the world's leading industrialists and they convene to decide how our lives are going to go. These are the boys who wrote the Alliance for Progress. They're the left wing of the ruling class.

They agreed with us on black control and student control. . . .

They want McCarthy in. They see fascism as the threat, see it coming from Wallace. The only way McCarthy could win is if the crazies and young radicals act up and make Gene look more reasonable. They offered to finance our demonstrations in Chicago.

We were also offered Esso (Rockefeller) money. They want us to make a lot of radical commotion so they can look more in the center as they move to the left."

THAT IS THE STRATEGY. THE LANDSCAPE PAINTERS FOCUS YOUR ATTENTION ON THE KIDS IN THE STREET WHILE THE REAL DANGER IS FROM ABOVE.

As Frank Capell recently observed in *The Review Of The News:*

"Of course, we know that these radical students are not going to take over the government. What they are going to do is provide the excuse for the government to take over the people, by passing more and more repressive laws to 'keep things under control.'"

126

The radicals make a commotion in the streets while the Limousine Liberals at the top in New York and Washington are Socializing us. WE ARE GOING TO HAVE A DICTATORSHIP OF THE ELITE DISGUISED AS A DICTATORSHIP OF THE PROLETARIAT.

Now the *Insiders* of the Establishment are moving into a more sophisticated method of applying pressure from below. John Gardner, a "Republican" and member of the C.F.R., has established a grass roots proletarian organization called Common Cause. This may become the biggest and most important organization in American history. Common Cause's goal is to organize welfare recipients, those who have not voted before, and Liberals to lobby for Socialism. That lobbying will not only be expressed in pressuring Congress to pass Socialist legislation but will also be expressed as ballot power in elections. Common Cause is supposedly the epitome of anti-Establishmentarianism, but who is paying the bills? The elite *Insider* radicals from above. The number one bankroller of this group to overthrow the super-rich and re-distribute their wealth among the poor is John D. Rockefeller III. Other key financiers are Andrew Heiskell (CFR), chairman of the board of Time, Inc., Thomas Watson (CFR), chairman of the board of IBM, John Whitney (CFR) of the Standard Oil fortune, Sol Linowitz (CFR), chairman of the board of Xerox, and Gardner Cowles (CFR) of Cowles publications. In any organization, the man who pays the bills is the boss. The others are his employees.

What better proof could we have that Socialism is not a movement of downtrodden masses but of power hungry elitists? The poor are merely pawns in the game. Needless to say, the landscape painters hide Common Cause's financial angels so that only those who understand that the Establishment's game plan is SOCIALISM understand what is going on before their very eyes.

CHAPTER EIGHT

YOU ARE THE ANSWER

Many people cannot refrain from rationalizing. After reading this book, some will bemoan the fact that the situation is hopeless. These will be many of the same people who, before reading this book, really did not believe the problems facing us were serious. Some people wake up and give up in the same week. This is, of course, just exactly what the *Insiders* want you to do.

The conspiracy *can* be defeated. The *Insiders* are not omnipotent. It is true that they control important parts of the federal government, high finance and the mass media. But they do not control everything, or the vise would already have been closed. We might say the conspiracy controls everything but you. *You* are their Achilles heel if you are willing to fight. There is an old cliche in sports that quitters never win and winners never quit. We need a million Americans who are *not* quitters, but, more-over, who have the will to win!

Of course, you can't buck the conspiracy head on. . . . trying to fight it on its home grounds. But the *Insiders* are vulnerable to an end run. You, and thousands of others like you can make an end run if you want to. It is our intention in this closing chapter to show why it can be done and how you can do it.

The timing for an end run has never been better. What Barry Goldwater said in 1964, people were willing to believe in 1968. Most people who voted for Nixon did so because he promised to balance the budget, not establish wage and price controls; slash government spending, not multiply it; cut welfare, not push for a guaranteed annual income; stand firm against the Communists, not lead the Red Chinese into the U. N.; build America's defenses, not continue to unilaterally disarm us; and stop aid and trade with our avowed Communist enemies, not double it. These were the issues which supposedly differentiated Nixon from Humphrey. Now we see that Nixon has repudiated his own promises and carried out those of his opponent. By 1972, millions of Americans will have concluded that there is little difference between the leadership of the two major parties. And more and more people are beginning to realize that there is a tiny clique of conspirators at the top which controls both the Democrat and Republican Parties.

The one thing these conspirators cannot survive is exposure. The *Insiders* are successful only because so few of their victims know what is being planned and how *Insiders* are carrying out those plans. Conspiracies can operate only in the dark. They cannot stand the truthful light of day. Once any sizeable minority of the American people becomes aware of the conspiracy and what it is up to, the many decades of patient planning and work by the *Insiders* in this country can be destroyed in an amazingly short period of time.

This job is largely a matter of getting others to realize that they have been conned and are continuing to be conned. You must become the local arm of the world's largest floating university. But before you can go to work, pointing out these conspiratorial facts to others, you must know the facts yourself. This book is designed to give you these facts, and can be your greatest tool. It is available on tape casettes* so that you can virtually memorize its contents by listening to it repeatedly while you are washing the dishes or driving to and from work. The concept of an army of individuals which is dedicated to exposing "the conspiracy" frightens the *Insiders* because it works outside the channels which they control.

Richard Nixon has said of the Republican Party: "We've got to have a tent everyone can get into." The Democrats have obviously believed that for a long time.

(*From Gary Allen Communications, P. O. Box 802, Arcadia, California 91106.)

But a Party must be based on principles or it has no justification for existence. Bringing Socialists into the Republican Party theoretically may broaden the base, but, in
reality, serves only to disfranchise those who believe in a
Constitutional Republic and the free enterprise system.

In 1972, the Republicans will try to make you forget
that Richard Nixon was elected on George Wallace's platform but has been carrying out Hubert Humphrey's. The
pitch will be "party unity." "If not Nixon then who?"
will be the typical response to complaints about Nixon's
actions. But unity with evil is evil. During the campaign
of 1972, Nixon will again *talk* conservatively while the
C.F.R.'s Democrat candidate will sound frighteningly radical in order to stampede you into accepting Nixon as the
lesser of two evils. The Establishment may even run its
John Lindsay or Eugene McCarthy as a far Left third
or fourth party candidate in order to split the Democratic
Party and re-elect Richard Nixon with a comparatively
small number of votes.

It is only logical that the *Insiders* will try to apply the
coup de grace against America through a Republican
President simply because most people cannot believe that
a Republican could be "soft on Communism" or would
jeopardize our liberty or sovereignty. The watchdogs tend
to go to sleep with a Republican in office.

Democrats and Republicans must break the *Insider* control of their respective parties. The C.F.R.-types and their
flunkies and social climbing opportunist supporters must be
invited to leave or else the Patriots must leave.

It is up to you to put the politicians on the spot and
make the C.F.R.-*Insiders* a campaign issue. This can be
accomplished easily by creating the base of thinking that
will oppose their positions. The Socialists must be forced
to gather into one party. The conspiracy doesn't want
the resultant clear distinction between party ideologies.
The *Insiders* want the issues between parties to be cloudy
and gray, centering on personalities, not principles. Neither
party can come out strongly against Socialism as long as

it is pushing Socialist programs. But that is the way the *Insiders* want it.

The issue, very simply, is the enslavement of you and your children. Just because many of these *Insiders* are theoretically Americans, don't think they will spare this country the terror they have brought to thirty others through their hired Communist thugs. To the *Insiders,* the world is their country and their only loyalty is to themselves and their fellow conspirators. Being an American means no more to them than being an honorary citizen of Bali would mean to you. It has not bothered their consciences one iota that millions of your fellow human beings have been murdered, including 50,000 of your own sons in Vietnam. In order to solidify their power in the United States they will need to do here the same thing they have done in other countries. They will establish and maintain their dictatorship through stark terror. The terror does not end with the complete take-over of the Republic. Rather, then terror just begins . . . for total, all encompassing terror is an absolute necessity to keep a dictatorship in power. And terror does not mean merely punishing the enemies of the New Order. Terror requires the murdering and imprisoning of people at random . . . even many of those who helped them come to power.

Those who are complacent and hope to escape the terror because they were not involved in politics or resisted the New Order coming to power must be made, by you, to understand that this all-encompassing need for terror includes *them* especially. . . . that they cannot escape by doing nothing.

What can we expect from the conspiracy during the next few years? Here are fourteen signposts on the road to totalitarianism compiled some years ago by historian Dr. Warren Carroll and a refugee from Yugoslavian Communism, Mike Djordjevich. The list is not in any particular order nor is the order of any particular significance as given here. But the imposition of any one of these new restrictions on liberty (none of which was in effect when

131

the list was compiled) would be a clear warning that the totalitarian state is very near; and once a significant number of them—perhaps five has been imposed, we can rationally conclude that the remainder would not be far behind and that the fight for freedom and the preservation of the Republic has been lost in this country.

FOURTEEN SIGNPOSTS TO SLAVERY

1. Restrictions on taking money out of the country and on the establishment or retention of a foreign bank account by an American citizen.

2. Abolition of private ownership of hand guns.

3. Detention of individuals without judicial process.

4. Requirements that private financial transactions be keyed to social security numbers or other government identification so that government records of these transactions can be kept and fed into a computer.

5. Use of compulsory education laws to forbid attendance at presently existing private schools.

6. Compulsory non-military service.

7. Compulsory psychological treatment for non-government workers or public school children.

8. An official declaration that anti-Communist organizations are subversive and subsequent legal action taken to suppress them.

9. Laws limiting the number of people allowed to meet in a private home.

10. Any significant change in passport regulations to make passports more difficult to obtain or use.

11. Wage and price controls, especially in a non-wartime situation.

12. Any kind of compulsory registration with the government of where individuals work.

13. Any attempt to restrict freedom of movement within the United States.

14. Any attempt to make a new major law by executive decree (that is, actually put into effect, not merely authorized as by existing executive orders).

As you are no doubt aware President Nixon already has invoked numbers 1, 11 and 14.

Steps 2, 3, 6, 7, 9, 12 and 13 already have been proposed and some are actively campaigned for by organized groups. As of January 1, 1972, banks must report to the government any deposit or withdrawal over $5,000. The next step will be to restrict the taking of money out of the country. Big Brother is watching your bank account!

Increased government control over many kinds of private schools is proposed annually in many state legislatures. Compulsory non-military service—a universal draft of all young men and women, with only a minority going into the armed services has been discussed by the Nixon Administration as an alternative to the draft. Sensitivity training is already required for an increasing number of government workers, teachers and school children. As long ago as 1961, Victor Reuther proposed that anti-Communist groups and organizations be investigated and placed on the Attorney General's subversive list. The propaganda war in progress to force registration or confiscation of firearms is the number one priority of all the collectivists—an armed citizenry is the major roadblock to a totalitarian takeover of the United States.

You are in this fight whether you want to be or not. Unless you are an *Insider,* you are a victim. Whether you are a multimillionaire or a pauper you have an enormous amount at stake.

The *Insiders* are counting on your being too preoccupied with your own problems or too lazy to fight back while the chains of slavery are being fastened on you. They are counting on their mass media to con you, frighten you, or ridicule you out of saving your freedom, and, most of all, they are counting on your thinking you can escape by not taking part in opposing their takeover.

They are also counting on those of you who recognize the conspiracy becoming so involved with watching all moves that you become totally mesmerized by their machinations, and thus become incapable of acting.

The choice is yours. You can say, "It can't happen here!" But nearly every one of the one billion people enslaved by the Communists since 1945 doubtless said the same thing. Or you can *end run* this whole conspiratorial apparatus.

The choice you must make was enunciated by Winston Churchill when he told the people of England:

> "If you will not fight for right when you can easily win without bloodshed; if you will not fight when your victory will be sure and not too costly; you may come to the moment when you will have to fight with all the odds against you and only a precarious chance of survival."

Because we have ignored warning after warning, we are now at that place in history. Unless you do your part now, you will face a further choice, also described by Mr. Churchill. He said:

> "There may be even a worse fate. You may have to fight when there is no hope of victory, because it is better to perish than live as slaves."

WHAT WILL YOU DO?

If you are unwilling to get involved because you feel it may be bad for business or may jeopardize your social respectability, just look into the eyes of your children and tell them that making a buck and climbing the social ladder are more important to you than they are.

This is the end of our case.

If you have decided not to do anything about it, then

you can close this book, read no further, and turn out the light. That is just what you will be doing for the United States of America, and may God help us. And may He have mercy on your soul.

If you decide that you *will* do something—that you at least are not yet controlled—*read on*—pick up the ball we are tossing you and with thousands of others, let's "end run" the conspiracy.

Here's how: The four keys in this program are:

1. *You.* What you do now is, of course, the key to this whole operation. If you delay, your motivation will wane, your concern will recede, but the danger will increase. Remember, the *Insiders* don't care how much you know about their conspiracy so long as you don't do anything about it. So keep reading and then act.

2. *This book: None Dare Call It Conspiracy.* In writing this book we have tried to give a concise overall picture of the nature of the conspiracy. We wrote it not only to explain the conspiracy, but to give you a complete program of *action* now, so that the many "You's" around the country would not necessarily have to be articulate salesmen to make your "end run." You can simply pass this book out and let it do the job for you. The conspiracy may be able to stifle publicity on this book and keep it off the magazine rack at your local supermarket, but they can't stop you from distributing it to friends, neighbors, relatives and business associates and especially in your precinct. With a potential 30 million distribution of this book to those mentioned above (and in a manner yet to be described), you will create a base of opinion that will throw the *Insiders* out.

It is quite possible that in distributing this book, questions will come up concerning certain statements and conclusions with which you are not able to deal. There are a number of organizations that have well documented material on all subjects raised in this book. But after considerable personal research the author has concluded that the organization which is the leader in this field, has had

135

the most experience, and is doing the best job of exposing the conspiracy is The John Birch Society.*

Doesn't it appear strange that this organization which works toward decentralization of political power and the exposure of the *Insiders* should be so vilified by the mass media, while the Council On Foreign Relations, which promotes centralization of power in the hands of a few within a world government, is practically never mentioned? So contact The John Birch Society for further back-up information (Belmont, Massachusetts 02178—San Marino, California 91108—or check your telephone directory for the nearest American Opinion Bookstore)

3. *Your Precinct.* The precinct is the lowest denominator in our political structure. Any politician will agree that whoever reaches and influences the most people in the precinct wins the election. When you break down the job to be done to this least common denominator, it doesn't seem to be nearly as big a job as when you look at those millions of votes that need to be switched. Many elections are won or lost by less than five votes per precinct. Remember that every vote-switch you can accomplish (by planting the seed with your book) really amounts to *two* votes, as it takes one from the other side.

Start your "end run" in your own precinct now. Lists of registered voters are available from your County Registrar. With everyone working within his own precinct, the hit and miss efforts of prior years will be avoided and organization will be added to this effort. A blanket coverage of your precinct will create talk between neighbors on this subject and thereby greatly increase the number of persons reading this book.

4. *Your Congressman.* You have now completed the three simple basic moves in your "end run." Barring a

---

(*The *Berkeley Gazette* stated in an editorial of August 26, 1971, commenting on The John Birch Society's 1958 ten point predictions for the United States, "Whatever Else, Call Him [Robert Welch] 'Correct.'" Write Box 8352, San Marino, Ca. 91108, for copy of editorial.)

wholesale awakening by the American people, it is probably wishful thinking to believe that the C.F.R.'s hold on the Presidency can be broken in 1972. But it is possible to block the *Insiders'* men in the House of Representatives. Congress can still lift a powerful voice against the conspiracy if only it would. It can also throw a searchlight on to the C.F.R.'s stranglehold on the executive branch of the government. No burglar tries to rob a house when a spotlight is on him. With your effort Congress can be that spotlight.

It is at the Congressional level that the conspiracy can be delayed at least until there is sufficient strength to rout it. But your local Congressional candidates must be *forced* to take a public stand on the Council on Foreign Relations, its goals, and its power in the federal government. And once your candidate is elected you must make sure that he does not submit to the incredible pressure which will be put upon him in Washington to compromise his principles. The Congressman for whom you are laying the base for election must be as steadfast in Washington as he is at home in personal conversation with you. Keep in mind that a Congressman must return to his constituents every two years for re-approval.

How would you like to be a Congressman who had voted for any one of the 14 Signposts to Slavery, asking to be elected by constituents who had read *None Dare Call It Conspiracy?* It is therefore easier to keep a Congressman on the straight and narrow than a Senator or the President. The latter run less frequently than Congressmen and represent tremendously larger geographical areas. Although it is not easy, it is still possible for a good Congressman to finance his campaign from within his district and not be dependent on the *Insiders* for campaign contributions.

If there are no Congressional candidates worth supporting in your area at this time, support one or more in other areas. *Never contribute money* to the Republican or Democratic National Committees. That money, except in token amounts, will never reach anti-C.F.R.-Establishment can-

137

didates, most of whom suffer from a severe shortage of funds, at least until they are well established. Only contribute your campaign dollars to those who are committed to fighting the conspiracy. A candidate running on good conservative principles is not enough. We've had many such candidates, and although most of them are very good men, they never come to grips with the real problems—exposing those behind the World Socialist Movement.

So, organize your "end run," pass out your books and then keep your eagle eye on your Congressman and his voting record.

This "end run" concept we are suggesting is not just a game we are playing even though we use a football term.

To summarize: You do not necessarily have to be an articulate salesman to make this "end run." You do not necessarily have to know all the in's and out's of the total conspiracy—the book is intended to do this for you.

All you have to do is find the wherewithal to purchase the books and one way or another see that you blanket your precinct with them. Then force your Congressman to stand up to the C.F.R. Establishment.

It is simple. It is straightforward. It is a workable plan.

With 30 million "end runs" being made during 1972, you can, and will, rout the conspiracy, turn the tide of history and prevent the enslavement of yourself and your family.

Remember, seeds planted in 1972 will pay off not only this year, but in 1974 and 1976. If we do not build a large counter-revolutionary base in 1972, the ball game will be lost by 1976.

MEMBERS OF THE COUNCIL ON
FOREIGN RELATIONS NOMINATED
AND APPOINTED BY PRESIDENT
NIXON TO GOVERNMENT POSTS

ADM. GEORGE W. ANDERSON, JR.,
Chairman, President's Foreign Intelligence Advisory Board

DR. GEORGE P. BAKER, Advisory
Council on Executive Organization

GEORGE BALL, Foreign Policy Consultant to the State Department

JACOB D. BEAM, Ambassador to the
Soviet Union

DAVID E. BELL, Member of the National Commission on Population
Growth and the American Future

LT. GEN. DONALD V. BENNETT,
Director of the Defense Intelligence
Agency

C. FRED BERGSTEN, Operations Staff
of the National Security Council

ROBERT O. BLAKE, Ambassador to
Mali

FRED J. BORCH, Member, Commission
on International Trade and Investment
Policy

DR. HAROLD BROWN, General Advisory Committee of the U. S. Arms
Control and Disarmament Agency, and
senior member of the U. S. delegation
for talks with the Soviet Union on
Strategic Arms Limitations (S.A.L.T.)

WILLIAM B. BUFFUM, Deputy Representative to the United Nations; Ambassador to Lebanon

ELLSWORTH BUNKER, Ambassador to
South Vietnam

FREDERICK BURKHARDT, Chairman,
National Commission on Libraries and
Information Service

DR. ARTHUR BURNS, Counsellor to
the President—later Chairman of the
Board of the Federal Reserve, succeeding C.F.R. member William McChesney Martin

HENRY A. BYROADE, Ambassador to
the Philippines

LINCOLN P. BLOOMFIELD, Member,
President's Commission for the Observance of the 25th Anniversary of
the U.N.

COURTNEY C. BROWN, Member, Commission on International Trade and
Investment Policy

DAVID K. E. BRUCE, Chief of the
U. S. Delegation to the Paris Talks

HARLAN CLEVELAND, Ambassador to
N.A.T.O.

RICHARD N. COOPER, Operations,
Staff of the National Security Council

PHILIP K. CROWE, Ambassador to
Norway

GARDNER COWLES, Board of Directors
of National Center for Voluntary
Action

WILLIAM B. DALE, Executive Director
of International Monetary Fund

NATHANIEL DAVIS, Ambassador to
Chile

C. DOUGLAS DILLON, General Advisory Committee of the U. S. Arms
Control and Disarmament Agency

SEYMOUR M. FINGER, Alternate to
the 25th Session of the General Assembly of the U.N.

HARVEY S. FIRESTONE, JR., Chairman of the Board of Governors,
United Service Organization, Inc.

WILLIAM C. FOSTER, General Advisory
Committee of the U. S. Arms Control
and Disarmament Agency

THOMAS S. GATES, Chairman, Commission on an All-Volunteer Armed
Force

CARL J. GILBERT, Special Representative for Trade Negotiations

GEN. ANDREW J. GOODPASTER, Supreme Allied Commander in Europe
(succeeding C.F.R. member Gen.
Lyman Lemnitzer)

KERMIT GORDON, General Advisory
Committee of the U. S. Arms Control
and Disarmament Agency

JOSEPH ADOLPH GREENWALD, U. S.
Rep. to the Organization for Economic
Cooperation and Development

GEN. ALFRED M. GRUENTHER, Commission on an All-Volunteer Armed
Force

JOHN W. GARDNER, Board of Directors, National Center for Voluntary
Action

RICHARD GARDNER, Member, Commission on International Trade and Investment Policy

T. KEITH GLENNAN, U. S. Rep., International Atomic Energy Agency

GORDON GRAY, Member, President's Foreign Intelligence Advisory Board; Member, Civilian Defense Advisory Council

MORTON HALPERIN, Operations Staff of the National Security Council

CHRISTIAN A. HERTER, JR., Commissioner on the part of the U. S. on the International Joint Commission —U. S. and Canada

REV. THEODORE M. HESBURGH, Chairman of the U. S. Commission on Civil Rights; Member of Commission on All-Volunteer Armed Force

SAMUEL P. HUNTINGTON, Task Force on International Development

JOHN N. IRWIN II, Special Emissary to Discuss Current U. S. Relations with Peru

J. K. JAMIESON, Member National Industrial Pollution Control Council

SEN. JACOB K. JAVITS, Rep. to 25th Session of General Assembly of U.N.

JOSEPH E. JOHNSON, Alternate Rep. to the 24th Session of the General Assembly of the U.N.

HOWARD W. JOHNSON, Member, National Commission on Productivity

JAMES R. KILLIAN, General Advisory Committee of the U. S. Arms Control and Disarmament Agency

WILLIAM R. KINTNER, Member of Board of Foreign Scholarships

HENRY A. KISSINGER, Assistant to the President for National Security Affairs, Chief Foreign Policy Advisor

ANTONIE T. KNOPPERS, Member of Commission on International Trade and Investment Policy

GEN. GEORGE A. LINCOLN, Director of the Office of Emergency Preparedness

HENRY CABOT LODGE, Chief Negotiator at the Paris Peace Talks

GEORGE CABOT LODGE, Board of Directors, Inter-American Social Development Institute

HENRY LOOMIS, Deputy Director of the United States Information Agency

DOUGLAS MacARTHUR II, Ambassador to Iran

ROBERT McCLINTOC, Ambassador to Venezuela

JOHN J. McCLOY, Chairman, General Advisory Committee of the U. S. Arms Control and Disarmament Agency

PAUL W. McCRACKEN, Chairman of the Council of Economic Advisors

EDWARD S. MASON, Task Force on International Development

CHARLES A. MEYER, Assistant Secretary of State

BRADFORD MILLS, President of Overseas Private Investment Corporation

FRANKLIN D. MURPHY, Member of the President's Foreign Intelligence Advisory Board

ROBERT D. MURPHY, Special Consultant on International Affairs

PAUL H. NITZE, Senior member, U. S. Delegation for Talks with the Soviet Union on Strategic Arms Limitations (S.A.L.T.)

GEN. LAURIS NORSTAD, Commission on an All-Volunteer Armed Force; Member, General Advisory Committee of the U. S. Arms Control and Disarmament Agency

ALFRED C. NEAL, Member, Commission on International Trade and Investment Policy

RODERIC L. O'CONNOR, Assistant Administrator for East Asia of the Agency for International Development

ROBERT E. OSGOOD, Operations Staff of the National Security Council

FRANK PACE, JR., Member of the President's Foreign Intelligence Advisory Board

RICHARD F. PEDERSEN, Counselor of the State Department

JOHN R. PETTY, Assistant Secretary of the Treasury for International Affairs

CHRISTOPHER H. PHILLIPS, Deputy Rep. in the U.N. Security Council

ALAN PIFER, Consultant to the President on Educational Finance

140

SEN. CLAIBORNE PELL, Rep. to 25th Session of the General Assembly of the U.N.

ISIDOR I. RABI, Consultant-at-Large to the President's Science Advisory Committee

STANLEY R. RESOR, Secretary of the Army

ELLIOT L. RICHARDSON, Undersecretary of State—now head of the Dept. of Health, Education and Welfare

JOHN RICHARDSON, JR., Assistant Secretary of State for Educational and Cultural Affairs

JAMES ROCHE, Board of Directors, National Center for Voluntary Action; Member, National Commission on Productivity

DAVID ROCKEFELLER, Task Force on International Development

NELSON A. ROCKEFELLER, Head of a Presidential Mission to Ascertain the Views of Leaders in the Latin American countries

RODMAN ROCKEFELLER, Member, Advisory Council for Minority Enterprise

ROBERT V. ROOSA, Task Force on International Development

KENNETH RUSH, Ambassador to the Federal Republic of Germany

DEAN RUSK, General Advisory Committee of the U. S. Arms Control and Disarmament Agency

JOHN D. ROCKEFELLER III, Chairman, National Commission on Population Growth and the American Future

NATHANIEL SAMUELS, Deputy Undersecretary of State

ADOLPH WILLIAM SCHMIDT, Ambassador to Canada

JOSEPH J. SISCO, Assistant Secretary of State for the Middle East and South Asia

DR. GLENN T. SEABORG, Chairman of the Atomic Energy Commission

GERARD SMITH, Director of the Arms Control and Disarmament Agency

HENRY DeW. SMYTH, Alternate Rep. of the 13th Session of the General Conference of the International Atomic Energy Agency

HELMUT SONNENFELDT, Operations Staff of the National Security Council

JOHN R. STEVENSON, Legal Advisor of the State Department

FRANK STANTON, U. S. Advisory Commission on Information

ROBERT STRAUSZ-HUPÉ, Ambassador to Ceylon and the Maldive Republic

LEROY STINEBOWER, Member, Commission on International Trade and Investment Policy

MAXWELL D. TAYLOR, Chairman, President's Foreign Intelligence Advisory Board

LLEWELLYN THOMPSON, Senior Member U. S. Delegation for talks with the Soviet Union on Strategic Arms Limitations (S.A.L.T.)

PHILIP H. TREZISE, Assistant Secretary of State

CYRUS VANCE, General Advisory Committee of the U. S. Arms Control and Disarmament Agency

RAWLEIGH WARNER, JR., Board of Trustees Woodrow Wilson International Center for Scholars

ARTHUR K. WATSON, Ambassador to France

THOMAS WATSON, Board of Directors, National Center for Voluntary Action

JOHN HAY WHITNEY, Board of Directors, Corporation for Public Broadcasting

FRANCIS O. WILCOX, Member of President's Commission for the Observance of the 25th Anniversary of the U.N.

FRANKLIN HAYDN WILLIAMS, President's Personal Representative for the Negotiation of Future Political Status with the Trust Territory of the Pacific Islands

WALTER WRISTON, Member, National Commission on Productivity

CHARLES W. YOST, Ambassador to the United Nations

OPERATION COUNTERATTACK

You can help! For every dollar you contribute Concord Press promises to mail out four books. Each one will go to a vital segment of America. The press, politicians, businessmen, doctors, lawyers, blue collar, white collar —all need to know. Our goal is thirty million copies sent to thirty million households. We can offer this low price because we use professional mass mailing services. In all probability four years from now you will not be able to distribute a book like this. It is only in a Presidential election year that masses of people are motivated to read such a book. It is now or never.

CONCORD PRESS
P. O. Box 2686
Seal Beach, Calif. 90740